Defenders of the Unborn,
Winners of Souls,
Christian Patriots

Defenders of the Unborn, Winners of Souls, Christian Patriots

A Victorious Sixty-Five-Year Journey Turning Ninety Thousand to Righteousness

Charles Kacprowicz

FOREWORD BY
Darrin Waldroup

RESOURCE *Publications* · Eugene, Oregon

DEFENDERS OF THE UNBORN, WINNERS OF SOULS, CHRISTIAN PATRIOTS
A Victorious Sixty-Five-Year Journey Turning Ninety Thousand to Righteousness

Copyright © 2024 Charles Kacprowicz. All rights reserved. Except for brief quotations in critical publications or reviews, no part of this book may be reproduced in any manner without prior written permission from the publisher. Write: Permissions, Wipf and Stock Publishers, 199 W. 8th Ave., Suite 3, Eugene, OR 97401.

Resource Publications
An Imprint of Wipf and Stock Publishers
199 W. 8th Ave., Suite 3
Eugene, OR 97401

www.wipfandstock.com

PAPERBACK ISBN: 979-8-3852-2421-0
HARDCOVER ISBN: 979-8-3852-2422-7
EBOOK ISBN: 979-8-3852-2423-4

VERSION NUMBER 08/16/24

Unless otherwise noted, all scriptures are from the KING JAMES VERSION, public domain.

Contents

Preface | vii
Foreword by Darrin Waldroup | ix

1. God's Knock at the Door | 1
2. Chasing Russian Communist Submarines and Communication Trawlers | 6
3. A Wife Perfect for Me | 14
4. Three Seductive Women and an Angel | 17
5. Seeking God's Direction | 21
6. Searching for God Purposes | 31
7. January 22, 1973—Day of Infamy | 39
8. Christians Are to Be Witnesses for Christ | 52
9. Steet Corner and Jail Ministries | 72
10. Restoring the Years | 79
11. Look Unto the Fields | 82
12. The Harvest and Blessings | 88
13. Are Christians Pacifists? | 91
14. Unborn Child Amendment | 99
15. Countermand Amendment | 111
16. Dietrich Bonhoeffer, Lutheran Pastor and Patriot | 120
17. My Wife's Final Days | 124

CONTENTS

18. Since My Wife's Death | 130
19. Redeeming the Time | 135

About the Author | 139

Preface

My wife of fifty-eight years, Joyce Eloise Casper, was in the last days of her life. For two years she suffered from a very aggressive strain of Melanoma Cancer. I was standing at the foot of her bed looking at a woman who was now a total invalid. She had no use of her arms, legs, neck or facial muscles. She was bald and as unattractive a woman I've ever seen. My heart pounded as the nurse was attending to her needs. I was holding back tears. Looking at my wife, I said to the nurse:

> 'I love this woman today more than I did when she first knocked my socks off.'

The nurse quickly looked at Joyce and said,

> 'Did you hear what your husband said?'

Joyce was unable to move or speak, but she did have the ability to blow air out of her mouth. She gathered her remaining strength and whispered, 'Yes'. My wife went home to be with the LORD a few days later.

PREFACE

At the suggestions of friends and by way of remembrance, I am writing these personal memoirs to encourage my readers in the LORD and to strengthen their faith and walk with Jesus Christ.

"All things are possible with God."
(Luke 1:37)

Foreword

Christian Patriots delves into the inspiring sixty-five-year journey of faith, resilience, and unwavering commitment to principles that define the lives of extraordinary individuals—Ray and Joyce 'Kacprowicz' Casper.

Through the lens of sixty-five years, this book traces the remarkable journey of Christian Patriots who have stood firm amidst adversity, triumphing over challenges, with steadfast conviction.

Their stories illuminate the power of faith, community, and unwavering dedication to a higher calling, inspiring readers to embrace their own journey with courage and hope.

Join us on a compelling exploration of faith, perseverance, and the enduring legacy of Christian Patriots.

Jesus NEVER Fails,

Dr. Darrin Waldroup
Author, Pastor, Evangelist
Titus 2:13-14

Chapter 1

God's Knock at the Door

"I now write unto you; in both which I stir up your pure minds by way of remembrance:" (2 Peter 3:1)

PUTTING THE PIECES OF one's life together from memory and then organizing them in a book is an enormous challenge. Foremost is the challenge of making certain that the LORD Jesus Christ is prominent and central to every personal, business and ministry event. Believing that the LORD is directing me to do so—here we go.

Growing Up in Jersey City:

My early life was somewhat uneventful. I was born in Jersey City, NJ in 1941, into an Italian Catholic community. My birth name is Raymond Charles Kacprowicz. My father changed our family name from Kacprowicz to Casper. These memoirs are written in my legal name 'Raymond Casper' and my 'Assumed Name' and 'Author's Name' which is 'Charles Kacprowicz'.

My father served in the Cavalry during the thirties. He worked as a Marine Machinist at the Brooklyn Naval Base. My neighborhood friends did what most boys do, they hung around the corner to talk and sometimes sing. Occasionally there would be fights among us, but we learned how to respect one other. I cannot remember when anyone was injured in a fight. When there was a threat against any one of us, the rest of the gang would come to his rescue. One evening, a rival gang drove by our corner and shot a zip gun at us. We all managed to duck. No one was hurt. It was a miracle that this attack did not develop into a gang war. There were occasional skirmishes between rival gangs.

On one occasion, my younger sister wanted to find out what her older brother and his friends were doing on the corner. The conversations among my friends were sometimes vulgar and when I saw my sister coming, I immediately chased her home. She of course was not happy with me. Today my sister is my trusted counselor and very special Christian friend.

World Events During My Early Years

In 1939, Nazi Germany made a ten-year non-aggression pact with the Soviet Union (Communist Russia). Hitler secretly agreed with Stalin that Germany would attack Poland from the West and Stalin would attack from the east. Poland was annihilated and squeezed into submission. Poland is my family's homeland. My Grandmother, along with family members migrated from Poland to the United States around 1900. My father traveled to Poland about 1919 after WW1 and returned nine years later. He lived with his sister who was married to a Polish Aristocrat.

During WW2, upwards of six million Poles were murdered by Hitler and Stalin. Millions more may have been made slaves, never to be heard from again. To this day, I ache inside thinking of what many of my ancestors suffered.

Beginning of My Christian Life

When I was about eight years old, my father and I were talking in the kitchen. We lived in a very small second floor, one-and-a-half-bedroom apartment. The size of the smaller bedroom was about twelve by fifteen feet. My parents managed to make room in this bedroom for my sister, two brothers and myself. We had a bunk bed on which I slept on the top bunk and my sister on the bottom. Our two younger brothers slept in a twin bed.

Every night my mother would gather us together to kneel at our bedside and say our prayers before going to sleep:

> 'Now I lay me down to sleep. I pray the Lord my soul to keep. If I should die before I wake, I pray the Lord my soul to take. And this I ask for Jesus sake, bless Mommy and Daddy, bless my sister and brothers, bless my aunts and uncles and all my friends. AMEN'

Over many years, the four of us recited this prayer nightly.

While Dad was talking with me, there was a knock at the door. Dad opened the door and there stood a man dressed in black with a white collar. He said he was Pastor Paul Hines from the St. Paul Evangelical Lutheran Church in Jersey City. My father asked him to come in.

Pastor Hines didn't delay in getting to the point. He said, 'Would you allow your eldest child, to come to Sunday School and Church on Sundays?' My Dad immediately said, 'yes'.

The LORD was now beginning a journey for my family that has thus far resulted in 90,000 people coming to know Jesus Christ as their Savior.

Foundational Years at St. Paul Evangelical Lutheran Church

The Church had a small congregation and was about 1 ½ miles from our apartment. At least twice a week, I would walk to Church with holes in my soles, on cement sidewalks, in rain or snow. I often stuffed cardboard in my shoes to keep my feet from contacting the sidewalk.

Pastor Hines mentored me for eight years. He took me through Lutheran Catechism classes and when I was fourteen years old, he brought me through my Confirmation. Mr. Frohm, a Church leader, taught me how to be a Boy Scout and Explorer. Pastor Hines also took my sister and two brothers through Catechism and Confirmation. Mr. Frohm mentored my two brothers through Cub/Boy Scout programs and campouts.

One Sunday morning, as I was listening to Pastor Hines' message, he challenged the entire congregation by declaring, 'We must serve Jesus!' I was sixteen at the time and said to myself, 'I don't know how to serve Jesus.'

Little did I know that the Lord would take my words and begin to build in me a great hunger to know and serve Jesus Christ. (Philippians 3:10)

About thirty-years later, I had a great desire to visit Pastor Hines at his Church to thank him for his unspeakable love and sacrifices that he made for my family. Sadly, when I got to his Church, I was told he was fired two weeks earlier. I asked where he lived and drove to his home. I knocked at the door. At first Pastor Hines did not recognize me. After telling him who I am, he invited me into his home. He had been arguing with his eighteen-year-old grandson. I began to explain why I was visiting him:

'Pastor Hines, I am here to say with the greatest sincerity, and on behalf of my siblings, how grateful we are that you snatched us out of a neighborhood that had no protestant Churches and no evangelical believers. In fact, we lived in a neighborhood where members of the Mafia resided.'

I shared with him how the LORD got a powerful hold on my life when I was thirty, and how He gave me a witness and ministry that has led my and my wife's families to the LORD. I told him we were also privileged to lead three hundred prisoners to the LORD—fifty of whom I baptized in the showers. Along the way there were many strangers and individuals in our extended families who came to know the LORD. All because you, Pastor Hines, mentored us for eight years.

He was tearing up. He looked over toward his grandson and asked me if I would talk with him. I did, but his grandson had no interest in hearing about Jesus, nor the glorious life of his grandfather.

I pray for the salvation of Pastor and Mrs. Hines' family and extended families, and Mr. and Mrs. Frohm's family and extended families till this day. I pray earnestly that not one of their family members would leave this planet without being saved.

I left thankful to God that I was able to tell Pastor Hines all that the LORD Jesus accomplished through my life, up to that time. Pastor Hines left a legacy for Jesus Christ through the Casper family that continues till this day. Pastor Hines died 6 months later.

> *'Bless you LORD for watching over us and guiding us even when we are unaware of your presence and purposes.'*

Chapter 2

Chasing Russian Communist Submarines and Communication Trawlers

The Korean War had ended, but there were rumblings that other conflicts were likely. Nanna, the uncle of one of my friends was killed in Korea, which left a deep impression on me. On leave from the Army, he would visit our neighborhood and ask one of us to hold onto his left arm and another on his right arm. He then swung us around and around. I learned to love Nanna very much.

Instead of being drafted, I decided to join the United States Navy. I was accepted shortly after I was 17 with my father's permission. I would finish active duty the day before my twenty-first birthday.

After finishing basic training at Great Lakes Naval Station Great Lakes, IL, I was sent to Radioman School for three months.

CHASING RUSSIAN SUBMARINES AND COMMUNICATION TRAWLERS

Serving on the USS Borie, DD 704

After nine months at the Naval Communications Station Cheltenham MD, I was transferred to the Destroyer USS Borie, DD-704. In 1945 the Borie was attacked by four Kamikaze pilots. One of them crashed into the superstructure of the ship—forty-eight men were killed and sixty-six wounded. The USS Borie was involved with many other campaigns after WW2—Korea, Vietnam, Bay of Pigs, Cuban Missile Crisis, rescue missions, to name a few. Borie participated in forcing a diesel-powered Russian submarine to the surface during the Cuban Missile Crisis, then offered the submarine aid and supplies. Borie, with two other destroyers, escorted the submarine out of the area. She was one of the Navy's lead Destroyers during the Cold War—1949 to 1972, when she was decommissioned.

My primary job as a Radioman on the USS Borie was to monitor and respond to radio communications (voice, teletype, and Morse Code) between ships in our squadron, coded messages to/from Naval Command and with ships from other nations.

Ordered to Fix a Rusty Shackle

Shortly after joining the USS Borie, I was ordered to climb up the mast, about two stories, and fix a rusty shackle. I grabbed a cable for support, but the shackle broke loose. As I began to fall, somehow, I had the presence of mind to hold on to the cable which caused me to fall in an arch, rather than straight down to the steal deck. Before slamming into a bulkhead, I let go of the cable and dropped about seven to eight feet onto the deck. A Chief was running toward me to cushion my fall. He didn't arrive in time. The Chief said, I bounced about two feet off the deck.

After a physical examination, I was summoned to Sickbay to sign my medical discharge papers. My back had not been bothering me, so I asked the Doc if I could finish my tour. He smiled and agreed. The medical discharge papers were cancelled.

Years later, I began having trouble with my legs and feet. Apparently, the nerves in my back were not sending correct signals to the lower part of my body. Over the last many years, my legs and feet became numb, my skin became tight, and my feet and legs became weak. I fell several times and foolishly thought I could tough it out. A dear friend asked me to visit a Disabled American Veterans Chapter three times. On the third invitation, I finally attended one of their meetings. DAV has since played an indispensable role in my life.

Accused of Being a Communist

While on board the USS Borie DD 704, some of the sailors were saying that I was a Communist because I was reading a book called 'The Soviet Crucible'. It wasn't long before the ship was buzzing with 'Casper is a Communist'. It would not have taken much, during one of our cruises into the Atlantic, to be flipped overboard. The Captain learned of this and called me to his Stateroom. He asked if I would let him see the book I was reading. I said 'yes, of course'. The next day he called me back to his Stateroom and said, 'I commend you for reading this book. I have put the word out that everyone on this ship is to get off your back.' He asked me to keep reading the 'Soviet Crucible' and other related books. After this, my shipmates were friendly. There were no more false accusations against me.

Liberty Requires Lifelong Vigilance

The USS Borie was continually monitoring activities in the Atlantic Ocean from the North Atlantic to South America. Our primary mission was to interdict Russian Communist Submarines and Communication Trawlers. The Borie was one of the ships involved in the Bay of Pigs Invasion and Cuban Missile Crisis.

Recollection

When I was sixteen years old, two representatives of Fidel Castro visited our neighborhood in Jersey City telling us that we needed to join Castro's revolution in Cuba. Neither myself, nor any of my friends joined the revolution. And now, 2 ½ years later, I was in the middle of a global struggle opposing Communist Russia's plans to install nuclear missiles in Cuba. Who would have thought?

Cuban Missile Crisis

I was not directly involved with the final standoff in the Cuban Missile Crisis. A month before, I was transferred to the USS Waldron. However, the USS Borie played a vital role in the blockade of Cuba. The Borie, and two other destroyers, ordered the Captain of a Russian submarine to surface because it was off the Florida coast and was part of Russia's plans to ship nuclear missiles to Cuba. When the Captain refused to do so, the USS Beale ordered a depth charge be dropped on the Russian submarine. The submarine's communication equipment was damaged, and the Russian Captain was unable to communicate with his Command Center.

Years later it was reported, by Moscow, that the Russian submarine was carrying nuclear weapons. The Russians had a rule, in such a circumstance, that three of their top Officers, on the submarine, must agree unanimously before their nuclear weapons could be released. One of the Officers, Vasili Arkhipov's, refused to allow the release of their nuclear weapons, arguing that we were not in WW3. Remember, this was happening at the time when President John F. Kennedy was threatening Moscow with nuclear retaliation if they did not remove their nuclear missiles from Cuba.

Communism: Evil Beyond Measure

While serving on the USS Borie, I developed a great interest in knowing why we were the good guys. I found a book, mentioned above, at the public library called the 'Soviet Crucible' by Samuel Hendel. The author was reporting the horrors that were happening at that very moment in the Soviet Union under Stalin. Mao Tse tung was also murdering millions in China.

Human Lives Murdered at the Hands of Totalitarian Governments

During the 20th Century, it is estimated that governments throughout the world murdered upwards of one hundred and fifty million people.

When it comes to mass murders by governments, communist regimes are the most lethal. The following estimates will vary depending on the source:

- People's Republic of China (1949 to 1987): Under Mao Tse tung and the Communist regime, upwards of eighty million people were murdered. As many as, three and one half million Chinese were murdered during the 1930's and 1940's by Communists.
- Soviet Union: During the course of its existence, it was responsible for a tremendous loss of life:
    a. Red Terror: up to three million died in the 1930's during political purges by Joseph Stalin.
    b. During the 1930's three and one half million Ukrainians were starved to death by Stalin.
    c. WW2 Soviet deaths: It is estimated that upwards of forty million Soviet soldiers and citizens died during WW2.

    "The heart is deceitful above all things, and desperately wicked: who can know it? I the LORD search the heart, I try

the reins, even to give every man according to his ways, and according to the fruit of his doings." (Jeremiah 17:9,10)

In My Lifetime

Looking back, it seems incredible that in my lifetime, so many of God's heritage (each man made in the image of God) were slaughtered by Satanic tyrants in defiance of the LORD's purposes for creating men.

I Don't Think She is Ready

While speaking with the mother of an eighteen-year-old, shortly after her daughter's birthday, I said, 'I don't think she is ready.'

The mother responded—'She'll be alright'.

'I told her, when I was eighteen, I was on a Destroyer steaming up and down the Atlantic Ocean chasing Russian Communist Submarines and communication Trawlers.

On two separate occasions, we were ordered to commandeer Russian Trawlers, and I was the boarding party's Radioman.

With each interdiction, we pointed our 5-inch guns at the Trawlers as the boarding party prepared to go down the rope ladder into a dingy. On both occasions, the Trawlers immediately steered a course out of our waters.

In the North Atlantic, temperatures would drop to 40 degrees below zero. Four inches of ice would cover the entire Destroyer. The sea's swells would reach 50 feet, completely submersing the ship from bow to stern. The Captain would be constantly balancing the angle of the ship to the swell to avoid capsizing. We would be fighting these seas for days.'

The mother answered, 'Well, I guess our kids need

to do much more growing'.

We Are in a Battle for Minds, Souls, and Lives of Men

Although this book's primary purpose is to share the soul winning testimonies of my wife and me over fifty-nine years, it is imperative that the reader grasp the fact that Christians, like it or not, are in the middle of the bloodiest battles in human history. We are engaged in life and death struggles for the minds, souls, and lives of men.

> "And I will put enmity between thee and the woman, and between thy seed and her seed; it shall bruise thy head, and thou shalt bruise his heel." (Genesis 3:15)

Contrary to what some Church leaders are saying, we are, in fact, living at the evilest time since Noah's flood. During the 20th and 21st Centuries, degenerate men brought genocide and infanticide into the world on a scale never imagined. I have knots in my stomach thinking how evil we have become. We have surely fallen to the bottom of the depravity barrel.

Mankind cares nothing that each human being, created by God, was purposed to be a member of His heritage. Christians should be jealous for God's heritage. I plan to say more about these tragedies later in the book.

> "Blessed is the nation whose God is the LORD; and the people whom he hath chosen for his own inheritance." (Psalm 33:12)

This much I can say, 'It has been very difficult to focus on bringing people to Jesus Christ while abortions, infanticide, genocide, and unspeakable atrocities, are happening all around us.' Add to this our personal adversities my wife and I suffered over fifty-nine years. But God has been faithful and has sustained us to carry out the work He assigned to us:

> "The Lord is not slack concerning his promise, as some men count slackness; but is longsuffering to us-ward, not willing that any should perish, but that all should come to repentance." (2 Peter 3:9)

God's Favor Has Been on America

A great part of this human carnage happened during the Cold War (1949 to 1991). God had given America the power (spiritual, economic, and military) to bring an end to the Soviet Union and Korean War. During the Cold War years, America had 300,000+ Churches (including para-Church Ministries), many hundreds of Christian schools, colleges, and universities, 400,000+ Preachers, thousands of Missionaries, and charities.

God has had His hand of favor on America because as a nation, we did not deny that Jesus Christ is the Son of God, and we enjoyed a Christian morality that God honored. During WW2, upwards of forty million Russian military and civilians were killed.

America had approximately 365,000 military members killed. We can see from these statistics that God's favor has been on America.

Are we now, since WW 2, witnessing God's hand of favor being removed? I am persuaded, the answer is—YES!

Chapter 3

A Wife Perfect for Me

AFTER MY TOUR IN the Navy, I moved to Los Angeles. Before starting College, I took a job with a manufacturing firm that wanted me to fly to Euclid, OH for a two-day training seminar. Dick, a fellow employee, was going with me.

Meeting My Wife

On the first night, Dick and I were having dinner in the hotel's restaurant. I noticed sitting at the counter two young women. One was a beautiful brunette. I said, 'Dick, do you see that brunette at the counter?' He said, 'Yes'. 'She's beautiful, don't you think?' He said, 'Yes'. I told him, 'I'm going over there to talk with her.' He replied, 'You can't just go over there. She won't talk with you. She doesn't even know your name.' However, I wasn't about to let his gibberish deter me.

I politely walked over and introduced myself. It was about 6:00 P.M. We started talking, and continued talking, and then we talked some more. 'No kissing.' We enjoyed a couple of dances and afterwards we began talking again. 'Still no kissing.' *I knew in my heart that this woman would become my wife.*

Before we knew it, it was 3:00 A.M. I said, 'Joyce, we need to meet again tomorrow before I leave for Los Angeles.' She said, 'Oh, I don't know, my Dad is going to be very angry.' Joyce was going to be twenty-one in four weeks, but she still lived in her father's house and wanted to honor him. She said, 'I will try to figure something out.'

She was able to plan for us to meet the next day. Again, we talked and danced for a while—no kissing. Just before I had to leave, I said, 'Joyce, we need to set a wedding date.' She was stunned, but never said no. She did say, 'That would take a longtime planning—maybe many months.' I said, 'then we need to get started right away.' I told her that, 'I could be back in three months to give her an engagement ring and that in the meantime, we could communicate by phone and in letters.' She agreed. Joyce had kept all my letters—I found them after she died. What a treasure of memories she left me.

Separated for Three Months

The thought of leaving her now, after only 24 hours together, troubled me greatly. The next three months would prove to be the longest months of my life. I would go to the mailbox hoping to find another letter. The LORD surely knew what He was doing when He created us male and female, and when he gave me Joyce Eloise Roschy to cherish for the rest of my life.

After a very long, lonely three-months, I flew back to Euclid, OH for a couple of days. We met with her parents, who gave us their blessing. I finally presented Joyce with an engagement ring. The long delay was over—I thought.

Joyce had been busy preparing for our wedding and scheduled it for three months later. I said to myself,

'Oh no, not another three months.'

Finally, the last three months had past, and I was flying back to Euclid for our wedding. Joyce and I are Polish, and she had prepared for a traditional Polish wedding.

> *'Oh LORD, how I love this woman and thank you for giving her to me over these 59 years.'*

Without Joyce, I don't believe the LORD would have given me 90,000 souls.

As I am recounting these events, I am in tears remembering how blessed I have been.

We were married on September 19, 1964, at a Catholic Church in Euclid, OH. After the ceremony, we were taken to the reception hall. There were maybe 350 people attending. There was a band, food, and beverages. Joyce and I danced to Polkas throughout the evening. It was a marvelous Polish reception. Friends and relatives came from many Eastern and Midwestern States. Sadly, it was also the last time I saw my Dad . . .

On the next day, Joyce and I headed off to Los Angeles on our honeymoon. Neither of us knew then what incredible plans the LORD had for the two of us.

Chapter 4

Three Seductive Women and an Angel

AFTER GRADUATING FROM COLLEGE and finishing one year of law school, Joyce and I were asking what's next. Our oldest son was born at the beginning of my first year at Law School. Joyce's income had stopped because she had to take care of our son. My VA Benefits also stopped. I tried to sell household items while in Law School, but early on, I developed pulmonary problems which drained me of physical and mental strength. A condition that plagues me to this day. Recently, the Veterans Administration has concluded that my symptoms were caused by Asbestos exposure on the USS Borie and two other Destroyers.

Learning to Walk With Jesus

Neither of us were walking closely with the LORD. However, we both agreed to move back to Euclid so our son could enjoy his grandparents and great grandparents. We packed our belongings and started back to Ohio.

A Special Truck Driver

I owned an automatic stick shift Volkswagen. Only three of the four cylinders were firing. On top of the car, we put our son's crib. Inside, there was barely enough room for me to fit into the driver's seat. Joyce flew to Ohio with our son. As I was driving across the country, I barely made it to the top of hills. One trucker knew what was happening and waited for me at the top of a hill. He wanted me to come behind him so I could catch his wake. He led me across much of the Mid-West. He was a very special trucker. Oh yes, I pray for this trucker and his family, even now, asking that all of them would be saved.

Offered a Partnership

It wasn't long before I was offered a partnership in an investment firm in Akron, OH—about 45 minutes from Euclid. I accepted. The firm catered to high-income individuals. The office was plush with rich thick carpets, mahogany framed walls, richly designed wallpaper, twelve-foot mahogany reception counter, eight-foot mahogany desk and work table with an eight-foot plush sofa in my Executive Office.

Hiring a Secretary

My first task was to hire a secretary. I called the Employment Agency and told them I needed a secretary who can take shorthand, type, and had administrative skills. They quickly sent over an attractive young woman who took shorthand, could type and had administrative skills. As I was interviewing her, she sat on my sofa in front of my desk. I could hardly not notice that she was wearing a mini skirt, and it left little to the imagination. I said to myself, 'This won't work.'

I called the Agency again and asked them to send me another candidate. I reminded them that the candidate needed to take shorthand, type, and have administrative skills. The next day the second candidate came to my office. She too was attractive and fully qualified. As I was sitting behind my desk, I began to interview her. It didn't take long to notice that she too was wearing a miniskirt which, again, left little to the imagination. Now I am getting frustrated.

I called the Agency, a third time, and asked them to send another candidate. They did. She too was qualified and attractive, but again wearing a miniskirt. Now I am fit to be tied. As a young man, all these interviews left fanciful notions swirling around in my head.

God's Secretary

I called the Agency for the fourth time and said, 'Look, I don't care if the candidate can take shorthand, or type, or have administrative skills. Just send me over an old lady.'

Little did I know, at the time, but the LORD was protecting me and my marriage so Joyce and I could serve Him and complete our ministry that would eventually lead 90,000 men and women to a saving knowledge of Jesus Christ.

In short order, an old lady of 60 years came to my office (remember, I was 30 at the time). She was pudgy, with a loosely fitting dress that dropped down her ankles. She was not able to take shorthand, she could not type, and she had no administrative skills. I thought to myself, maybe I could teach her how to be the secretary I needed. When the interview was over, I looked at Anna, straightway, and said, "ANNA, YOU'RE HIRED."

Anna's Ministry to Me

From the first day Anna came to work, she carried with her a Bible. She made it a habit to leave it on her counter, in full view of anyone entering the office. After a few days, she asked me if I would like to attend a Bible Study that she and some friends were having on Wednesday night. I politely said no.

About two weeks later, with her Bible conspicuously sitting on her counter, she asked again, would I like to attend her Bible Study this Wednesday night? Again, I said no.

A couple of weeks later, she asked me a third time, but this time I figured I'd better say, yes—maybe she would stop asking me, 'Yes Anna, I will come Wednesday night.'

When I walked into the home hosting the Bible Study, I was stunned. Here were seven older folks (remember I'm only thirty), each holding their Bibles and reading passages to each other. They would make comments about what the LORD was saying and explained how it applied to them. I quickly developed a deep respect for these people. Yes, I did have early training in the importance of the Bible and Bible Doctrine, but these people elevated my knowledge and interest in the LORD to a much higher level. I attended Anna's Bible Study, faithfully, for five years.

Anna's Legacy

Anna (God's Angel) has since gone home to be with the LORD. But today, I pray for her family, and extended family, asking God not to allow even one of them leave this planet without Jesus Christ. I truly love Anna, more than my words can say. God used her to set me on a path that has changed the lives of many people, especially mine.

> *Thank you, LORD, for leading me to Anna's Bible Study. Thank you for your love, patience and mercy toward me and my family.*

Chapter 5

Seekings God's Direction

EVEN THOUGH JOYCE ATTENDED Church with me and our son faithfully, and she honored my decision to have a nightly Bible Study after dinner, I was greatly troubled that she may not know Jesus Christ as her personal Savior. She showed no interest in my schooling at Moody Bible Extension Studies, nor ministries that the LORD was directing me to pursue.

My prayer for Joyce

I pleaded with the LORD to give me a Christian wife. My prayer was: 'Lord, I don't care the cost—you can take my arm, even my life—but please, confirm to me Joyce's salvation.'

Confronting My Wife

One evening before Joyce fell asleep, I stood at the foot of the bed and said,

'Joyce, many centuries ago, there was a man by the name of Joshua who stood before the people of Israel and said,

> "... choose you this day whom ye will serve; ... but as for me and my house, we will serve the LORD." (Joshua 24:15)

We know from scripture that Joshua's wife did not rebel against his decision. Neither did his children.

As your husband, I am telling you that as for me and my house—we will serve the LORD. Now, you have to decide if you are going to go the way of feminists inside and outside the Church and destroy our family, or if you will decide to honor the LORD, and your husband, and allow God to teach us how to follow Him together.'

Joyce's Conversion

Nearly one and a half years later, I was appointed to lead a fellowship group from our Church. There were about twenty people attending. I asked them to sit in a circle, and starting on my left, tell everyone what Jesus means to them. As they began sharing their testimonies, about halfway through the circle, it occurred to me that Joyce really had no personal testimony to share about Jesus. I surely didn't want to embarrass her. I was thinking of terminating the meeting.

Suddenly, Joyce stood up and spoke to the group. She said she was now a born-again Christian, and that she asked Jesus to forgive her of her sins, and to become her Savior about two weeks earlier. I was stunned. The group praised the LORD. Although Joyce kept her decision from me for two weeks, I was elated that God answered my prayer.

Joyce, a Gem Among God's Best

Joyce, over the years, became one of the finest and most respected Christian ladies in the Church.

Before and after her conversion, she took care of me, our two sons, daughter-in-law, eight grandchildren and many others outside our family. The LORD used the disciplined training she received in Catholic school to become a most trusted wife and faithful Christian servant.

Shortly after confirming her salvation, she was asked to be the Director of Pioneer Girls. She came to me and said, 'I am not qualified to lead this ministry of one hundred girls. I have no training or experience to be their Director.' I said sweetheart, the LORD will show you all you need know and besides, the only way for Christians to grow, in their faith, is to be ministering to others.

Joyce accepted the leadership role in Pioneer Girls, and she and her girls grew in the LORD greatly. At the end of the first year, she was asked to give her report from the pulpit to the Church. She was nervous and said she was not a public speaker. However, she gave her report, and it was excellent. The Church showed much appreciation for her labor. Her girls bragged on her as they shared their experiences during the year. It was a wonderful moment for me too. To see 'my wife' publicly sharing the LORD's work in her life was overwhelming.

Stopping Abortion, Restoring Our Christian Heritage, and Constitutional Republic

After Roe v. Wade was decided in 1973, I knew the LORD was directing me to go forward with what was to become the *Article 5 'Unborn Child Amendment'*.

We looked for support from Churches, Congress and State Legislators for fifty-one years. We found no interest in an Article 5 'Unborn Child Amendment'.

During the last nine years of our marriage, we continued our labors to restore our Constitutional Republic and Christian heritage with the *Article 5 Countermand Amendment*.

Since 1971, the LORD used us to turn many hundreds of people to a saving knowledge of Jesus Christ through Jail Ministry, Bible Studies, Street Ministries, Public Speaking, One on One Witnessing, etc.

Throughout these years, I had the added burden of having to earn a living for our family, ministries, and initiatives:

My Wife and I Suffered Terribly

Early on, I was becoming greatly burdened for the souls of men.

> "For the love of Christ constraineth us; because we thus judge, that if one died for all, then were all dead. And that he died for all, that they which live should not henceforth live unto themselves, but unto him which died for them, and rose again." (2 Corinthians 5:14,15)

Joyce and I attended Church three times a week, I led Bible Studies, taught Sunday School, became involved in Church leadership, visited the sick, directed a Jail Ministry, plus ministered to our immediate and extended family.

During these years, we also advanced the Unborn Child Amendment in Congress and 200+ Churches, the Countermand Amendment in thirty-eight State Legislatures, and Ministry Channels International.

In addition, we operated businesses that we thought would fund our efforts.

Over five decades, Joyce and I suffered many loses and hardships:

1. 3 home foreclosures,
2. loss of multiple cars,
3. 3 business failures,
4. treasures lost,
5. bankruptcies,

6. the loss of $5 million in cash,
7. Initial Public Offering for $1 million in 1987, cancelled two days before funding. Stock Market collapsed,
8. Initial Public Offering for upwards of $100 million in 2001, cancelled a few days before funding. Stock Market collapsed,
9. Many personal/family issues,
10. Joyce's aggressive strain of Melanoma cancer that took her life—April 25, 2023.
11. my heart surgery, 5-bi-passes—January 3, 2020.

Moving to a New Church

My family, nineteen years ago, moved to another County in North Carolina. We attended a new Church for about a year. Joyce invited the Pastor and his wife over for dinner. We talked about many things, including the murder of Unborn Children and the responsibility of men to stop it.

Refused Membership in a Local Church

The next morning, my family and I were scheduled to become members of this Pastor's Church. A few minutes before the service began, the Pastor asked me to come with him to a private office. He told me that we would not be accepted into membership. I said nothing to him. I walked to the pew my family was sitting in and said, 'Joyce, we are leaving.' There were seven in my family to be accepted into membership that morning.

I do not know the reason why the Pastor rejected me and my family into membership, but his decision did hurt each one of us for some time.

The LORD led us to another Church where we have been members for eighteen years.

Identical Twins—Adopted as Their Grandpa

On the first Sunday attending our new Church, I heard of an unspeakable tragedy. A young father, whose wife six months earlier gave birth to identical twins, had killed himself while under the influence of drugs. He managed to call his parents screaming for help. His father called 911 and drove as fast as he could to help him. When he arrived, his son was dead, having just blown his head off with a shotgun.

Joyce and I attended his funeral and were heartbroken to see his wife holding their two six-month-old babies in her arms standing in front of his coffin. My first granddaughter was also six-months old at the time.

We were in tears just imagining what this mother and family were going through. I determined, at that time, to do whatever I could to encourage, pray and support this family. Over the years, our relationship grew. Soon, the twins were calling me grandpa. This is a title I am proud of, and it has stuck with me even till this day.

There have been other members born to this family since then. The LORD has blessed Joyce and me with the privilege of seeing our adopted family grow over the years.

Each setback left me with a terrible sense of helplessness. I often wondered why the LORD was allowing these catastrophes, when we were trying to follow His leading in the local Church, ministries, and initiatives.

> "Now the just shall live by faith: but if any man draw back, my soul shall have no pleasure in him." (Hebrews 10:38)

Why I Love My Wife

I love my wife dearly!

After a crisis, I would try to console her by putting my arms around her, giving her a gentle hug, kissing her on the cheek, telling her softly, that I greatly loved her and wouldn't trade her for a thousand others. I would tell her, 'I did not know what the LORD was doing, but I was confident He had not abandoned us.' I would say, 'Joyce, the LORD is confirming to us that He has not left us by virtue of the souls and ministries He keeps sending our way.'

I often told her that the LORD had given us a ministry that few Christians will have in their lifetime.

With each new convert, we were strengthened and afterwards we would pray asking the LORD to direct us to where He wanted us to go next.

> "Yea doubtless, and I count all things but loss for the excellency of the knowledge of Christ Jesus my Lord: for whom I have suffered the loss of all things, and do count them but dung, that I may win Christ." (Philippians 3:8)

> "Trust in the LORD with all thine heart; and lean not unto thine own understanding. In all thy ways acknowledge him, and he shall direct thy paths." (Proverbs 3:5,6)

Joyce Grew Less Confident in Her Husband's Business Decisions

As the years rolled by, decisions had to be made regarding ministries, businesses, family matters, income needs, etc. Joyce grew less and less confident that her husband knew what he was doing.

Before I proceeded with an idea that I thought might be the way the LORD was leading us, I would ask Joyce what she thought.

She would usually say, 'I don't know anything about that.' My response, 'I am not asking for a professional opinion. I just want to know what my wife thinks I should do?' I think because of the many times my decisions failed, she was gun shy and would finally say (except once), 'I don't like it.'

Her answer would leave me perplexed. I felt, as the husband in the family, Director of Ministries and Director of Initiatives, the LORD wanted me to do something. I still had the responsibility of providing for my family, and yet, I often had no clear direction from the LORD.

After much prayer, and committing the matter to the LORD, I would make a decision. Sometimes, I would decide that my wife's 'I don't like it.' was the one to follow. At other times, I felt compelled to go forward with the project I was praying about. Remember, most of the time, we had no steady income.

A few times my decisions were successful, but most of the time they failed. The failures were the ones that brought much grief to my wife and family.

Neither of Us Knew Where We Were Going

My burden for the souls of men, the Unborn Child Amendment, and Countermand Amendment weighed heavily on my heart.

Over the years, I was trying to follow the LORD by trusting Him to direct my steps. My wife was trusting the LORD through her husband's leadership. Neither of us knew where we were going.

Bragging on My Wife

You may wonder why I brag on my wife and love her so?

After every decision I made, that later failed, Joyce never once said to me, 'I told you so.' She would again join me in prayer, and we would ask the LORD's direction.

Joyce always supported the work I decided to pursue, even though earlier she said, 'I don't like it.' God's great miracle, in all this chaos, has been the fact that the LORD greatly blessed our lives, marriage, family, and ministries. BLESS YOU LORD! AMEN!

The LORD's ways are surely not our ways.

> "For My thoughts are not your thoughts, Nor are your ways My ways," says the LORD. For as the heavens are higher than the earth, so are my ways higher than your ways, and my thoughts than your thoughts." (Isaiah 55:8,9)

Advice From a Friend

A family friend recently told me, 'Maybe you should have listened to your wife's 'I don't like it.' As I pondered my answer, I said, 'If I did, would we have 90,000 souls who we led to Jesus?

My family friend acknowledged that she had not thought about that.

The Virtues of a Noble Woman

> "Who can find a virtuous woman? for her price is far above rubies. The heart of her husband doth safely trust in her, so that he shall have no need of spoil. She will do him good and not evil all the days of her life. She seeketh wool, and flax, and worketh willingly with her hands... She girdeth her loins with strength, and strengtheneth her arms... She stretcheth out her hand to the poor; yea, she reacheth forth her hands to the needy.... her clothing is silk and purple. Her husband is known in the gates, when he sitteth among the elders of the land. Strength and honour are her clothing; and she shall rejoice in time to come. She openeth her mouth with wisdom; and in her tongue is the law of kindness. She looketh well to the ways of her household, and eateth not the bread of idleness. Her children arise up, and call her blessed; her husband also, and he praiseth her.

> Many daughters have done virtuously, but thou excellest them all. Favour is deceitful, and beauty is vain: but a woman that feareth the LORD, she shall be praised. Give her of the fruit of her hands; and let her own works praise her in the gates." (Proverbs 31:10-31)

Three Reasons Why We Must Walk by Faith

It took a while, but I learned three important reasons why the LORD never tells us how to get to where He is leading us:

1. If He told me, surely, I would find a way to foul it up.
2. If He told me, surely, Satan would find a way to foul it up, and
3. If He told me, He would be violating the first principle of the Bible:

   > "Now the just shall live by faith: but if any man draw back, my soul shall have no pleasure in him." (Hebrews 10:38)

Joyce and I kept our sanity and Christian compass with each new unsaved person the LORD sent us. The LORD would also send us couples to minister to, individuals who were despondent, young ones who needed prayer and direction. With each new encounter, we were strengthened and realized the LORD had not abandoned us.

> "I will never leave thee, nor forsake thee." (Hebrew 13:5)

> 'Every man has to make his own way in life, but he also has to live in the consequences of his choices.'

Chapter 6

Searching for God Purposes

MY YEARS IN COLLEGE were unsatisfying. Yes, I did graduate and was accepted at Loyola Law School, but inside, I was feeling empty. I was expecting something better and yet I did not know what.

Learning at Anna's Bible Study

Anna's Bible Study became more meaningful to me as time went on. The Hostess, Mrs. Elizabeth Horn, took me under her wings and through prayer and Godly counsel encouraged me to continue my studies at Moody Bible Extensions Studies. She also recommended Joyce and I join Stow Alliance Fellowship at Stow, OH. Mrs. Horn quickly became my spiritual mother. What a lovely Christian woman. A beautiful gem among God's best.

Geri Burk, a Dear Friend for Life

Geri Burk was a member of Mrs. Horn's Bible Study. She contracted Polio at 18-years of age. Both her legs were paralyzed until her death at 86. Every day she had to attach steel braces, on both legs, in order to move about with her cane. Nationwide Insurance hired her as a receptionist in Akron, OH. She retired from Nationwide and continually sought ways to serve others and the LORD.

As the decades flew by, Geri and I would call each other several times a year. I was hurting for the suffering she was experiencing every day. I tried to drive to Ohio from North Carolina as often as possible. Watching her—alone—struggling to get through each day was difficult.

The most remarkable part of Geri's personality was the fact that every time we talked, before I could say anything, she would ask, 'How is Joyce? . . . How are your sons and grandchildren? . . . How was I doing? . . . How's your ministry?'

Geri reminded me that she prayed daily for me, my family, business, ministry, and initiatives. A few years ago, she fell and struck her head. She is home with the LORD now. I have been a very privileged Christian man to have had this beautiful, graceful, prayer warrior on my side for many decades. I love her much and miss her greatly.

Moody Bible Extension Studies

I took Mrs. Horn's recommendation to heart and became a student at Moody Bible Extension Studies for three and a half years. The focus of those years was to discover how our LORD's plan of redemption, throughout the ages, through Jesus Christ the Son of God, was presented in 66 books of the Bible, by as many as 44 authors.

It was time to pay for one of my semesters at Moody. Joyce and I were broke. I just quit a sales job in order to grow a business I thought had promise. We were behind with our rent and groceries. Joyce said, 'Raymond, you need to quit your schooling.'

Now the doubts began to emerge. I told Joyce, the LORD wanted me to continue in my schooling at Moody. She argued that we don't have enough money to pay for your tuition. I told her we must trust the LORD to provide for us.

There was a stack of mail on my counter that I hadn't looked at for weeks. As I began to thumb through it, I noticed a letter from my previous employer. I opened it and found a check for my expenses that had not yet been paid. The check was almost to the penny what I needed for tuition. This was an object lesson for the both of us. In short space, the LORD also provided the money we needed for our family and ministry.

> *"All scripture is given by inspiration of God, and is profitable for doctrine, for reproof, for correction, for instruction in righteousness: That the man of God may be perfect, thoroughly furnished unto all good works." (2 Timothy 3:16,17)*

Bill Herman, a Christian Friend Who Was Closer than a Brother

One Sunday, as I was attending worship services, a young man by the name of Bill Herman sat next to me in my pew. He had heard of the work I was doing with the Unborn Child Amendment and Evangelism. He lived in Columbus, OH, about one hundred miles from Stow, OH.

Bill told me he wanted to meet the man who is trying to stop abortion. I don't know how he heard of me, but our meeting was one of the greatest blessings of my life. I don't think it was more than a year after Roe v. Wade.

This unexpected meeting, at Church, began a fifty-year Christian friendship—better than King David's and Jonathan's. Bill stuck closer to me than a brother:

> *"... And there is a friend that sticketh closer than a brother." (Proverbs 18:24)*

Five decades ago, he began praying daily for me, my ministries, businesses and family. He counseled me many times.

We spent time together canvassing businesses looking for supporters for the Unborn Child Amendment. On one occasion, we visited a beauty salon. The beautician was taking care of a customer. When we introduced ourselves as Directors of the Article V Unborn Child Amendment Initiative, the owner yelled out: 'Where have you guys been?'

You see, Christian women, from 50 years back, have been praying for Christian men to step up and stop the slaughter of God's heritage.

The evil practice of abortion is out of the pits of hell. God gave Christian men, in America, the Constitution and the authority necessary to stop this infanticide permanently with the Article 5 Unborn Child Amendment.

One day his wife called telling me that Bill fell from a latter and broke his back in multiple places. I wept with her on the phone, realizing Bill had been seriously injured. He would be a complete paraplegic the rest of his life. Bill went home to be with the LORD two years ago. I miss him terribly. Yes, the LORD has given me many other wonderful friends, but Bill stands out because he cared for the souls of men and the Unborn Child. He supported my work and never expected to be compensated.

> *LORD JESUS, please comfort Bill's wife in her extended care facility and bless greatly every member of his immediate and extended family. Please don't let any of them leave this life without knowing Jesus.*

Stow Alliance Fellowship, the Beginning of a glorious Walk with Jesus

Joyce, still remembering her Catholic background, did not want to go to Stow Alliance. We finally agreed to compromise, one week we would attend a Catholic Church and the next Stow Alliance. However, after we attended a service at Stow Alliance Fellowship, Joyce no longer wanted to go to a Catholic church.

Stow Alliance gave us the grounding we needed in our Christian faith and marriage. Pastor Paul Valentine took five years to complete a study in 1st and 2nd Corinthians. These two epistles cover about every problem and sin Christians will experience in their Churches and families, and they provide us with God's solutions to all of them.

Jesus, Please Teach Me to Walk Closely

Because of what I was learning at Anna's Bible Study, Moody Bible Extension Studies and at Stow Alliance Fellowship, I was under deep conviction. My understanding of what it means to walk with Jesus had been sorely lacking.

In 1971, I prayed asking God to teach me who Jesus really is, and what I needed to do to walk closely with Him. Under great conviction, I confessed my sins anew (both hidden and overt), repented of all of them, and asked for God's forgiveness in the name and by the blood of Jesus Christ—the Son of God the Father. This prayer instantly confirmed my sonship with God (Born-Again through the death, burial and resurrection of my Savior Jesus Christ.) I have never looked back.

Learning to be a Husband and Father

In a very short time, I came to realize that I didn't even know how to be a Christian husband, or father.

I promised the Lord, if He would have my wife sit still at the supper table after dinner, I would read the Bible to my family. To my astonishment, Joyce began sitting at the dinner table the very first night I started reading the Bible. I began, of all places, at Genesis 1:1. Even my 2-year-old son would sit still as I read the Bible. Imagine talking about Genesis with your 2-year-old son. However, the LORD honored my prayer for my wife, even though she did not participate in discussions for maybe a year and a half. Miraculously, we continued our family custom of having a nightly Bible Study after dinner for 25 years. We read through the entire Bible several times.

The Marriage Vow

One day, I drove Joyce to an Optometrist for her eye exam. As I waited, a young attendant, who knew at time that we were married for fifty years, said, 'How did you and Joyce stay together for so long?' She was to be married in two weeks.

I thought for a minute and said, 'The cement that holds a marriage together is not love.' She looked at me startled. 'The cement that holds a marriage together is the 'vow' we take before the LORD, witnesses, and each other, acknowledging that we have promised to be married till death do us part.

1. Love adds sweet flavor to the marriage. At first, we are infatuated with each other.
2. As we get a little older, we start to realize our partner has flaws. The vow we made, before God, reminds us that our marriage is until death do us part.
3. Finally, when we are seniors, we enter a new relationship that is built on mutual love and admiration. This love is based on our loyalty, faithfulness, fidelity, and respect for each other. We held together all these years, because Joyce and I considered our vow before the LORD unbreakable.

"What therefore God hath joined together, let not man put asunder." *(Mark 10:9)*

Hatred of Sin and Burden for Souls

Early on, the LORD placed a great burden on my heart for the souls of men. I said two simple prayers:

1. LORD, please teach me to hate sin like Jesus hates sin. He has been working on me ever since; and
2. Please, do not allow me to see death until I have led and least 1,000 souls to a saving knowledge of Jesus Christ. Now at the time, I did not know 1,000 souls were a lot. All I knew was, I wanted to reach as many as possible for Jesus during my lifetime.

> *"but other fell into good ground, and brought forth fruit, some an hundredfold, some sixtyfold, some thirtyfold." (Matthew 13:8)*

Later in this book, I plan to talk more about how God used us to lead many to righteousness. For right now, I would like the reader to keep in mind that I asked God for 1,000 souls. He did not give me 1,000—He gave me 90,000 in seventy four nations. *To this day, I don't know why He used me in this way.*

> 'Bless you, thank you, praise you LORD, for your unspeakable love and goodness to us.'

My Vow to the LORD for My Son and Family

One night, I entered my two-year-old son's room. He was sleeping in his crib. I offered a prayer to the LORD that Satan, on many occasions, has used against me.

> 'LORD, I promise to raise my son to be like Jesus. Please, show me how to do this. If by prospering in business, the wealth would keep my son from being the Christian man you want him to be, then you have my irrevocable

> *commitment not to allow me to prosper. In Jesus name I offer this prayer.'*

(This prayer would extend to my entire family.)

During times when Joyce and I were suffering financial losses, I would remember my vow on behalf of my two-year-old son. Is this God's way of telling me that He is not pleased with my vow? Is my vow confirmation that the LORD was protecting my son by preventing me from prospering. Does He want me to take my vow back and maybe then I would begin to prosper?

Satan would somehow make my moments of misery even worse by impressing on me the idea that by rescinding my vow, I would surely prosper.

After hours of agony, I found myself, during every catastrophe, telling the LORD that if my vow is to be broken, then, He would have to break it. I would not take it back!

My son's and family's walk with the LORD was much too important to God and me.

Chapter 7

January 22, 1973—Day of Infamy

> *"But seek ye first the kingdom of God, and his righteousness; and all these things shall be added unto you."* (Matthew 6:33)

ON JANUARY 22, 1973, I was listening to the evening news. The United States Supreme Court had just decided in its Roe v. Wade decision, that America's mothers would now have the Constitutional Right to abort their Unborn Children in their wombs with impunity—God, the father, and America were to have no say in the mothers' decisions.

I knew, because the highest Court in the land was now condemning innocent Unborn Children to death, that God's favor toward America would be removed and His wrath would fall on us in its place.

> *"As for my people, children are their oppressors, and women rule over them. O my people, they which lead thee cause thee to err, and destroy the way of thy paths."* (Isaiah 3:12)

I have found myself praying, weeping and fasting before the LORD, that He would stop this atrocity and restore America to a God-fearing people once again.

United States Supreme Court—Seven Justices Who Will One Day Wish They Were Never Born

Seven of nine Justices granted this unconstitutional right (so called Constitutional), that they based on an unenumerated privacy right that is not mentioned in the Constitution. Prior to Roe v. Wade, all fifty States gave the mother privacy rights during her pregnancy. She just never had a right to murder the child in her womb.

American Women Took Pride in Presenting Their Baby to Their Husbands

It should be noted that American women, before 1973, cherished their Unborn Children and with joy presented the live baby to their husbands with pride. Both parents would love their new baby and care for him/her the rest of their lives.

My mother, when she was close to delivering me, told the Doctor, if he can only save one of us, he should save her son. I was never told what the medical problem was, but apparently the Doctor told my mother that there was a complication that could be dangerous to her and her baby. During the 1940's, American women thought it was a privilege to deliver their Unborn Children into the world. She saw this as her sacred duty to deliver into the world a new generation.

Today, we have allowed anti-male, anti-God, Marxist and self-worshiping feminist to deceive our women to believe Satan's lie that her situation and career justifies murdering her Unborn Baby with impunity. God will not be mocked. He will call to account everyone who believes this lie and who destroyed His purposes for nearly eighty million unborn babies in America.

> "Be not deceived; God is not mocked: for whatsoever a man soweth, that shall he also reap." (Galatians 6:7)

The Joy of a Live Birth

One evening, after work, my wife asked me to sit down because she had something important to tell me. I thought, at first, she had a serious problem. Then she said, 'Raymond, we are going to have a baby.' (notice the 'We') It was a wonderful moment for both of us.

Our Founders Acknowledged Our Dependence on Providence

The Founders, of our Constitution, acknowledged their dependence on a transcendent God who intervenes in the affairs of men and nations. They believed in the concept of Providence, which refers to God's most holy, wise, and powerful preservation and governance of all creatures and their actions. They saw no contradiction between our constitutional government and faith in God's providential care.

> "Thou shalt not kill." (Exodus 20:13)

> "Whoso sheddeth man's blood, by man shall his blood be shed: for in the image of God made he man." (Genesis 9:6)

Without God's Word, Our Constitution Is Just Another Piece of Paper

In essence, both the Declaration of Independence and the Constitution recognize the role of divine Providence in shaping the destiny of the United States. They declare the importance of relying on higher principles and guidance. Without the Word of God, and men living by its teachings, our Constitution is just another piece of paper.

The LORD knows our future by His foreknowledge, whether it be for nations or individuals. He gives men volition (free will) to choose their way, but He knows the consequences of their choices before they happen.

> "And hath made of one blood all nations of men for to dwell on all the face of the earth, and hath determined the times before appointed, and the bounds of their habitation;" (Acts 17:26)

> "For whom he did foreknow, he also did predestinate to be conformed to the image of his Son, that he might be the firstborn among many brethren." (Romans 8:29)

Our Founders knew these scriptures and designed our sacred documents with the LORD's purposes in mind.

Note: In the signature section of our Constitution, the Founders acknowledged Jesus Christ by giving the following, "in the Year of our Lord one thousand seven hundred and eighty-seven".

God's Redemptive Plan

For 3,500 years, God has been completing His plan of redemption through a little rivulet of humanity called Israel. It will be on the LORD's throne, at Jerusalem, where Jesus Christ will receive His regal scepter to rule the nations. Jews have been looking for their Messiah for 3,000 years—Christian's know Him as the Savior of mankind—Jesus Christ.

The Gospel Goes West

When Paul the Apostle to the Gentiles heard the Macedonian Call, he had no idea why the Holy Spirit, on two occasions, kept him from going east with the Gospel. When he heard the Call from Macedonia, asking for help, he knew it was from Jesus. He obeyed and started a Gospel journey that has lasted nearly 2,000 years. The Gospel that he took to Greece, he eventually took to Rome. Other Christians took it to Spain, France, Germany, England, America, Canada, South America, Africa, China, Southeast Asia, Philippines, New Zealand, Australia, and other nations.

When England was colonizing the nations, the LORD used their exploits to plant the Word of God, with the Gospel, throughout the world.

There were also Christians who took the Gospel East, but it did not take root like in the West.

God's Redemptive Purposes for Men Will Not Be Defeated

God's redemptive purposes, for mankind, were not to be defeated. He intended for the Gospel to penetrate millions upon millions of hearts in all nations of the world and in every generation. The miraculous fact is, He is still completing His plan of redemption through the choices of angels (both good and evil), and men (most of whom have no knowledge what God is doing though their decisions).

> *"The Lord is not slack concerning his promise, as some men count slackness; but is longsuffering to us-ward, not willing that any should perish, but that all should come to repentance." (2 Peter 3:9)*

Atrocities By Men

Yes, there have been unspeakable atrocities committed by men in every generation. God has suffered this because He gave men volition. Without volition, men would simply be robots obeying the will of God, without personal accountability. The LORD receives no pleasure from robots—however, through men who know His Goodness, worship Him in spirit and truth and obey Him willingly, He is well pleased.

In spite of the sinful nature of men and angels, God is propagating His Gospel to the nations, which is the only hope men have of ever being delivered from their sin and everlasting separation from God in hell.

> "So shall My word be that goes forth from My mouth; It shall not return to Me void, But it shall accomplish what I please, And it shall prosper in the thing for which I sent it." (Isaiah 55:11)

> "For God so loved the world, that he gave his only begotten Son, that whosoever believeth in him should not perish, but have everlasting life. For God did not send His Son into the world to condemn the world, but that the world through Him might be saved." (John 3:16,17)

Our Founders knew that Providence was guiding them. They understood that they were part of a much bigger plan that the LORD was advancing through their deliberations for America.

United State Supreme Court Condemned America by Authorizing the Murder of Unborn Children

These seven Supreme Court Justices were not God-fearing men. They made it open season on the Unborn Child—God's heritage.

They authorized, so far, the surgical murder of sixty-three million Unborn Babies in America. Millions more have been aborted non-surgically. The Court ignored the Preamble (first paragraph) in the Constitution which clearly protects the life of Unborn Children.

> Preamble to the Constitution
>
> "We the People of the United States, in Order to form a more perfect Union, establish Justice, insure domestic Tranquility, provide for the common defence, promote the general Welfare, and secure the Blessings of Liberty to ourselves and our **Posterity**, do ordain and establish this Constitution for the United States of America."

God's Righteousness v. Roe v. Wade

On January 23, 1973, while I was preaching in downtown Akron, OH—I cried out:

JANUARY 22, 1973—DAY OF INFAMY

'We must reverse Roe v. Wade. We must not give American women the right to decide who lives or dies in America.'

To my knowledge, I was the first man to speak out, publicly, against abortion. The first legal abortion had not yet been performed.

In Matthew 6:33 the LORD tells us that Jews and Christians have two primary missions on earth:

1. Seek God's kingdom by leading others to a saving knowledge of the Jewish Messiah—who Christians know as Jesus Christ, the Son of God; and

2. Seek God's righteousness in every area of our personal, political, governmental and social lives. Just because a politician, or feminist, or secularist (or even a Christian leader) says that abortion is a social, or political issue, Christians are duty bound to deny them their lies and deceptions and declare (with God's righteous authority) that the Unborn Child is a person deserving of the same protections born citizens have. We should also do battle with Satan's emissaries and endeavor to remove laws and Court decisions that allow God's heritage to be destroyed.

It is righteousness, when practiced and enforced in our homes, communities, Churches, and governments that makes it possible for men to live in peace and enjoy their families.

Abortion Destroys the Unborn Child—God's, America's and the Father's Heritage

For five plus decades, America's Unborn Children have been hunted down and murdered with scalpels, poisons, dissections, and abortifacients. Every year, 20% of live healthy Unborn Children are destroyed in the name of license, convenience, pleasure, idols, careers, etc.

50% of all adult women in America have aborted a baby in their womb. Feminism in America has become a cancer that has destroyed the family and incalculable future generations.

A mother can now have a medication abortion (mifepristone and misoprostol) up to seventy-seven days (eleven weeks) after the first day of her last period. Beyond that, doctors recommend a surgical abortion. How evil and cold-hearted we have become.

> "Be not deceived; God is not mocked: for whatsoever a man soweth, that shall he also reap." (Galatian 6:7)

Warnings From God

America was established, beginning with the Mayflower Compact in 1620, on God's righteous teachings from the Word of God.

God's righteous and biblical principles undergirded our local, State and national governments. We used to teach our children right from wrong. Today, only a small part of our population lives by the LORD's righteous teachings.

> "Hear the word of the LORD, ye children of Israel [America]: for the LORD hath a controversy with the inhabitants of the land, because there is no truth, nor mercy, nor knowledge of God in the land. By swearing, and lying, and killing, and stealing, and committing adultery, they break out, and blood toucheth blood. . . . My people are destroyed for lack of knowledge: because thou have rejected knowledge, I will also reject thee, that thou shalt be no priest to me: seeing thou has forgotten the laws of thy God, I will also forget thy children. As they were increased, so they sinned against me: therefore, will I change their glory into shame." (Hosea 4:6,7)

The LORD has given America many warnings of the judgments to come for having legalized the murder of His heritage and for removing His Word from our schools, workplace, and government. The spiritual void that has been left, empowers the LORD's enemies to ruin our Christian heritage, and with-it future generations that will follow after evil, rather than the LORD.

> *"Train up a child in the way he should go: and when he is old, he will not depart from it." (Proverbs 22:6)*

> *"Surely at the commandment of the LORD came this upon Judah, to remove them out of his sight, for the sins of Manasseh, according to all that he did; And also for the innocent blood that he shed: for he filled Jerusalem with innocent blood; which the LORD would not pardon." (2 Kings 24:3,4)*

America's Declension Started Before Roe v. Wade

America began its' moral and spiritual decline before Roe v. Wade in 1973:

1. Engel v. Vitale

    On June 25, 1962, the U.S. Supreme Court in Engel v. Vitale decided that a state prayer could not be mandated for recitation in public schools at the beginning of each school day, even if the prayer was denominationally neutral and students had the option to remain silent or be excused from the room.

    > *"So then every one of us shall give account of himself to God." (Romans 14:12)*

    > *"The fool has said in his heart, "There is no God." They are corrupt, They have done abominable works, There is none who does good." (Psalm 14:1)*

2. Abington School District v. Schempp

    In 1963, in Abington School District v. Schempp, the Court decided that school sponsored Bible reading and the recitation of the Lord's Prayer in public schools were unconstitutional under the First Amendment.

Both decisions marked the beginning of a frontal attack on America's Christian heritage, and the God-fearing values that the LORD, in generations past, honored by making America the world's leading military and economic power.

America—Witness to the Nations

America's Christian heritage and witness to the nations is an extension of the witness the LORD commanded Israel to carry out—to be a light to the Gentiles.

> "I the LORD have called thee in righteousness, and will hold thine hand, and will keep thee, and give thee for a covenant of the people, for a light of the Gentiles; To open the blind eyes, to bring out the prisoners from the prison, and them that sit in darkness out of the prison house." (Isaiah 42:6,7)

> "Blessed is the nation whose God is the LORD; and the people whom he hath chosen for his own inheritance." (Psalm 33:12)

> "And Jesus came and spake unto them, saying, All power is given unto me in heaven and in earth. Go ye therefore, and teach all nations, baptizing them in the name of the Father, and of the Son, and of the Holy Ghost: Teaching them to observe all things whatsoever I have commanded you: and, lo, I am with you alway, even unto the end of the world. Amen." (Matthew 28:18,19,20)

A Decision Out of the Pits of Hell

The greatest destruction of human life during the 20th and 21st Centuries has been the slaughter of Unborn Children in the womb:

- Since 1973, sixty-three million American babies have been murdered surgically in the womb.
- Millions more were killed non-surgically.

- Even though the United States Supreme Court has recently rescinded Roe v. Wade, there are still upwards of 3,000 Unborn Children being slaughtered and poisoned in the womb every day in America.

- Worldwide, it is estimated that 750+ million abortions have been performed.

- Worldwide, there may be 50,000+ abortions every day.

Utter and Complete Diabolical Evil!

A Christian's Duty to Every Generation

When Christians pray asking the LORD to bless America and restore us to a great nation once again, I am persuaded very few prayers are pleading with the LORD to forgive us of our personal and national sins.

Yes, Jesus will forgive every sin men commit, but first, the sinner must confess the sin, repent of it, and ask God to help him not to commit those sins again.

God's grace is sufficient to forgive us and sustain us when we are tempted, but He won't forgive our sins if we do not acknowledge them and repent of the evil we are practicing. This truth applies to both our personal and national sins.

America needs a Spirit led national revival. It can only happen when God's people, with confession and weeping, plead with the LORD, to cleans us of our filthy evil practices (personal and national), especially the destruction of our Unborn Children. Until the Church enters the righteous battles for the minds, souls, and lives of men, America will never see the restoration of our Christian heritage.

> *"If my people, which are called by my name, shall humble themselves, and pray, and seek my face, and turn from their wicked ways; then will I hear from heaven,*

> and will forgive their sin, and will heal their land."
> (2 Chronicles 7:14)

America's cup of iniquity is about full. Without the Church asserting its authority to protect God's righteousness in America, we will continue to quench God's Holy Spirit and He will move further away from America.

> "Quench not the Spirit." (1 Thessalonians 5:19)

> LORD JESUS, we are an undone people who do not know the right hand from the left. As only you can, please bring conviction upon your Church, forgiveness of our iniquities, and a personal and national restoration of our Christian heritage. AMEN!

Daniel's Prayer of Repentance is the Prayer America Needs at this Critical Hour

> "Then I set my face toward the Lord God to make request by prayer and supplications, with fasting, sackcloth, and ashes. And I prayed to the Lord my God, and made confession, and said, O Lord, great and awesome God, who keeps His covenant and mercy with those who love Him, and with those who keep His commandments, we have sinned and committed iniquity, we have done wickedly and rebelled, even by departing from Your precepts and Your judgments. Neither have we heeded Your servants the prophets, who spoke in Your name to our kings and our princes, to our fathers and all the people of the land. O Lord, righteousness belongs to You, but to us shame of face, as it is this day—to the men of Judah, to the inhabitants of Jerusalem and all Israel [United States], those near and those far off in all the countries to which You have driven them, because of the unfaithfulness which they have committed against You.

> "O Lord, to us belongs shame of face, to our kings, our princes, and our fathers, because we have sinned against You. To the Lord our God belong mercy and forgiveness, though we have rebelled against Him. We have not

JANUARY 22, 1973—DAY OF INFAMY

obeyed the voice of the Lord our God, to walk in His laws, which He set before us by His servants the prophets. Yes, all Israel [United States] has transgressed Your law, and has departed so as not to obey Your voice; therefore the curse and the oath written in the Law of Moses the servant of God have been poured out on us, because we have sinned against Him. And He has confirmed His words, which He spoke against us and against our judges who judged us, by bringing upon us a great disaster; for under the whole heaven such has never been done as what has been done to Jerusalem.

"As it is written in the Law of Moses, all this disaster has come upon us; yet we have not made our prayer before the Lord our God, that we might turn from our iniquities and understand Your truth. Therefore the Lord has kept the disaster in mind, and brought it upon us; for the Lord our God is righteous in all the works which He does, though we have not obeyed His voice. And now, O Lord our God, who brought Your people out of the land of Egypt with a mighty hand, and made Yourself a name, as it is this day—we have sinned, we have done wickedly!

"O Lord, according to all Your righteousness, I pray, let Your anger and Your fury be turned away from Your city Jerusalem [America], Your holy mountain; because for our sins, and for the iniquities of our fathers, Jerusalem and Your people are a reproach to all those around us. Now therefore, our God, hear the prayer of Your servant, and his supplications, and for the Lord's sake cause Your face to shine on Your sanctuary, which is desolate. O my God, incline Your ear and hear; open Your eyes and see our desolations, and the city which is called by Your name; for we do not present our supplications before You because of our righteous deeds, but because of Your great mercies. O Lord, hear! O Lord, forgive! O Lord, listen and act! Do not delay for Your own sake, my God, for Your city and Your people are called by Your name." (Daniel 9:3-19)

Chapter 8

Christians Are to Be Witnesses for Christ

Since 1971, the LORD has been teaching me how to lead strangers to Jesus. Here are a few of my witnessing experiences.

> *"For the Son of man is come to seek and to save that which was lost."* (Luke 19:10)

MY CHRISTIAN TESTIMONY BEGINS TO GROW

A Jewish Woman Receives Jesus Christ on Her Death Bed

About this time, I was working for a manufacturing company. My Christian testimony was being noticed by some. Our office secretary asked me to visit with her Jewish mother who was on her death bed and unsaved. I agreed and went to the hospital to visit her. As I walked into her dark room—I felt the presence of demons and the atmosphere was eerie. Mrs. Sepos was lying on her bed. She was functional and lucid. I immediately called on Jesus to rid the room of the presence of demons. Within moments, the oppressive atmosphere was gone. I walked toward the bed introducing myself to Mrs. Sepos. After a few introductory comments. I asked her what she would say to the LORD if He took her life tonight and asked by what right do you have to come into His heaven? She became very agitated. I knew my presence was upsetting her. I prayed over her asking the LORD's mercy. Realizing that Mrs. Sepos was not ready to talk with me, I left and told her I would try to come back later.

A couple of days later I visited her again, only this time she was terminal, having suffered a stroke. The room, however, was 'not' dark and eerie. She was no longer able to move or talk. She did understand me when I talked to her, and she was able to move the fingers in her left hand.

I asked her to squeeze my hand once, with her fingers, if her answer was yes to any of my questions. If no, squeeze it twice.

I asked her if she remembered my last visit. She squeezed my hand once. I asked her if she remembered the question: 'What right do you have to come into my heaven?'. She squeezed my hand once. I again told her that the Bible tells us that we are all sinners and separated from a Holy God. She squeezed my hand once. I asked her if she was ready to confess her sins to the LORD and ask to be forgiven. She squeezed my hand once. I asked her if she would repeat after me the following prayer by squeezing my hand once in response. She squeezed my hand once.

> LORD Jesus, I am a sinner separated from a Holy God. [She squeezed my hand once.]
>
> LORD Jesus, I confess my sins and repent of them, and I ask you to forgive me. [She squeezed my hand once.]
>
> LORD Jesus, please come into my life and make me a child of God. [She squeezed my hand once.]
>
> LORD Jesus, please help me to follow you for the rest of my life. [She squeezed my hand once.]

> LORD Jesus, thank you for saving me and making me a child of God. [She squeezed my hand once.]

Mrs. Sepos went home to be with Jesus as a completed Jew a few days later.

> *Thank you, LORD, for your immeasurable love and mercy.*

A Stranger Practicing 'Cutting' Comes to Christ

One day, on my way home, I stopped at a McDonald Restaurant. There was a disheveled man sitting on a bench. He just walked about a mile to McDonald's from the hospital he was treated at. He had suffered a serious leg injury. I greeted him thinking I would minister to him as I was leaving the restaurant.

Inside the restaurant there was a woman sitting in a fetal position with her head between her legs. She was in great distress. I asked her if I could help. She didn't answer. I asked her if she was hungry. She said, 'Yes'. I told her I would be back with her meal. I gave her a tract and asked her to read it. When I got back with her food, she looked at me and said, 'This (pointing to the Christian tract I gave her) is what I really need.'

Prayerfully, I led her through the sinner's prayer and asked if she wanted to start a new life. She said, 'Yes'. She confessed her sins, and asked Jesus to forgive her, and become her Savior. Astonishingly, she had five or six deep cuts on both arms. I asked her, 'What are these?' She said, 'She is a cutter.' I had no idea what a cutter was. Apparently, there is a sect that requires deep cuts in their bodies during religious ceremonies. I told her that she is now a child of God and must not cut herself anymore. There was a noticeable difference in her demeanor, and I attributed that to the fact that God's Holy spirit was already teaching her about her importance to God. She told me that she will no longer cut herself.

She said, 'She was waiting for someone to pick her up from Charlotte'—nearly two hundred miles away. I gave her $20 to help her.

She was now in tears and asked me, before I left, if she could give me a hug. Of course, I said, 'Yes'. I don't think she wanted to let me go. I committed her to the LORD and went on with my business.

A Disheveled Man Outside the Restaurant

Outside the restaurant there was still sitting on a bench the man who just came from the hospital. I asked him if he knew Jesus as his Savior and he said, 'Yes'. However, he was stranded and hungry. As I recall, I bought him some food and gave him $20 also. Since he had no transportation, I drove him to his unkept single wide mobile home about 5 miles away. I committed him to the LORD, and as I was leaving, he said, 'You didn't have to do this.'

Joyce's Grandma and Family Come to Jesus

One evening, Joyce and I were visiting with her grandparents. Grandma was sitting with us at the kitchen table. Grandpa was in the living room within listening distance. Both were exceptional grandparents. Grandma was always welcoming, no matter what time it was. Occasionally, I played Pinnacle with them for hours.

I said Grandma, if the LORD decided to take your life tonight and he asked: 'Helen, by what right do you have to come into my heaven?' What would you say?

Grandma thought for a moment and said, 'I never thought of that question.' I pressed her a little bit, 'Based on what you do know about God, what do you think you would say.' She thought again for a moment and said, 'Well, I would say I had the priest over once a week, I gave to charities, I didn't curse, I prayed, I was kind to my neighbors, I took care of my family.'—then she stopped.

I said, 'Grandma, is there anything else you would say to the LORD?' She said, 'I can't think of anything.' I asked, 'Would you like to know what the LORD would say?' She said, 'Yes'. I quoted her Matthew 7:21-23

"Not everyone that saith unto me, Lord, Lord, shall enter into the kingdom of heaven; but he that doeth the will of my Father which is in heaven. Many will say to me in that day, Lord, Lord, have we not prophesied in thy name? and in thy name have cast out devils? and in thy name done many wonderful works? And then will I profess unto them, I never knew you: depart from me, ye that work iniquity."

I asked her if she would like me to tell her what I would say? She said, 'Yes'. Her husband was listening from the living room.

'LORD, in and of myself, I have no right to come into your heaven. 'I can't work my way in, nor can I pay my way in. There is nothing I can offer that would cleans me of my sin. However, when I was on the earth, I believed you when you said, I was a sinner separated from a Holy God, and helpless to remove the sin barrier between us. I believed that Jesus Christ, your Son, paid the penalty for my sin by the shedding of His blood. I confessed my sins, repented of them, and asked you to forgive me in Jesus' name. I invited Jesus to take the throne of my life and I prayed that you would make me a child of God. At that moment, you forgave me of my sins, and I became part of the family of God. Based on your promises LORD, you will receive me into heaven. '

Grandma looked at her husband and said, 'Johnny, Ray is right! Ray is right!' However, neither of them, at this time, made a decision to receive Jesus Christ as their personal Savior.

Six months later, Grandma became ill and was bedridden. Her prognosis was not unto death. I was asked to stay with her one night.

In the morning, as I was walking by the foot of her bed, she called out to me and asked, 'Raymond, do you remember that question you asked me some time ago?' I said, 'Yes'. She looked at me, with troubled eyes, and said, 'Would you ask it again? I said, 'Of course'.

When I finished repeating the questions and what the LORD might say: 'Helen, by what right do you have to come into my heaven?', Grandma began weeping. As tears were flowing down her face, she loudly declared: "JESUS REDEEMS US!"

She was no longer depending on visits from the priest, her good works, or payments for her salvation. She was now a child of God by faith, through the Grace of God and the shed Blood of our Savior, Jesus Christ. By faith she believed God, and today she lives eternally in the halls of heaven. AMEN!

About two weeks later, Grandma went home to be with the LORD. She was seventy-eight years of age. I was able to lead her husband to the LORD a few weeks later. Joyce's sisters and mother came to know the LORD also.

> "But Jesus beheld them, and said unto them, With men this is impossible; but with God all things are possible." (Matthew 19:26)

Joyce's Father Rejects Salvation by Faith

Joyce's Dad was terminally ill with cancer. Surgeons opened him up and said they could not finish the operation because the cancer had metastasized. They sewed him back up and sent him home.

When we heard of his condition, Joyce and I drove from North Carolina to visit him in Florida. We took him and his wife to their favorite fish fry restaurant. My wife was greatly burdened for her Dad's salvation and tried to explain what Jesus did for her. He was irate and refused to let her talk. He said, 'I was going to Church before you were born.' Joyce was deeply hurt because of her Dad's rebuke. I was stunned. Joyce's Dad and I were not good friends. I was afraid to say anything that would inflame the situation more.

I was immensely proud of my wife. Yes, she was hurt deeply because of her father's anger and rebuke, but she was not ashamed to tell her father that Jesus Christ was her Savior. Thank you, LORD, for the powerful testimony you gave Joyce. THANK YOU, THANK YOU, THANK YOU LORD!

A few weeks later, her father died and likely went to a devil's hell.

Coming to Know Jesus in a Parking Lot

Last year, as I was parking my car, a young man came up behind me and said, 'I need your help.' I recognized him, but I did now know why he wanted to talk with me. He explained that he had been on an emotional roller coaster. He has not been sleeping well and has been unable to control his thoughts, especially sexual desires with women. We talked for a while and then he said, 'I know you are a Christian man and I want to be saved. Can you help me.' I said, 'Yes.', and led the young man in the sinner's prayer. I called on the LORD to save my brother and to rid him of these desires that are keeping him from having peace with himself and with God. The young man was gloriously saved on the parking lot. Today he is a born-again believer and member of the Family of God. AMEN!

Seven months later, the young man walked up to me and acknowledged that he was a child of God. He said his nightmares were not controlling him as before.

God Sends Me a Young Jewish Man

One day, I was sitting at a McDonald's Restaurant when a young man, about eighteen years of age, asked if I would drive him to the Square. I said, 'Yes'. We both got into my car and headed toward the Square. On the way, I learned the young man's father was Jewish, and mother was a Jehovah Witness.

I said to him, 'Do you not know that Israel is the most important nation on the planet.' He said, 'No'. I replied, 'God is completing His plan of redemption through the Jewish people and that tiny nation of Israel. The Mesiah, who your people are waiting for, Christians know as Jesus Christ.' His interest peaked. I asked him if he would like to be a completed Jew. He willingly said 'Yes'. I led him through the sinner's prayer and committed him and his family to the Lord. After he asked Jesus to forgive him of every sin, I welcomed him into the Family of God.

I told him it was extremely important that he ask the LORD to show him a Bible preaching Church that he can join.

A few months went by. He spotted me at the same restaurant. I asked him if he had found a good Church to attend. He said, 'No', but he was looking. About a year later he ran up to me and said, 'I found a good Church that I am attending.' I was overwhelmed by God's faithfulness.

My last words to him: 'We must now pray earnestly for your Mom and Dad that they too will come to know Jesus and be saved.' I suggested ways that he can grow in the LORD, and how he might be a good witness to his family.

An 11 PM Knock on MY Door

On occasion, my son would send one of his friends to talk with me about Jesus. One evening, at 11 pm, there was a knock on my door. He said, 'My son had sent him.'

I invited him in and asked why he wanted to see me. He said, I have many problems and I need your advice. After talking with him for an hour, I asked him if he wanted a fresh start in life by asking Jesus Christ to forgive him of his sins. He said, 'Yes.'

We both knelt in front of my sofa, and he gave his heart to the LORD and was gloriously saved. This young man is still my friend till this day.

A Divided Marriage

A couple, with a young daughter, were at each other's throats. They both said they were Christians. I had known both of them for some time and had been greatly troubled by their marriage breaking up.

I offered to meet with them and try to help remove their bitterness toward each other. They agreed. We all sat around a coffee table, looking at each other. I probed a bit, hoping they would open up. They did. I love the two of them very much:

The husband complained that his wife had no interest in his needs and was deliberately disgracing him. The wife said, 'Her husband was not showing her any attention and hardly ever saw him.'

I let them vent for a while, and then asked them to hear what the LORD has to say. They said, 'Yes'.

> "**Wives**, " *submit yourselves unto your own husbands, as unto the Lord. For the husband is the head of the wife, even as Christ is the head of the church: and he is the saviour of the body. Therefore as the church is subject unto Christ, so let the wives be to their own husbands in every thing."*

> **Husbands**, *"love your wives, even as Christ also loved the church, and gave himself for it; That he might sanctify and cleanse it with the washing of water by the word, That he might present it to himself a glorious church, not having spot, or wrinkle, or any such thing; but that it should be holy and without blemish. So ought men to love their wives as their own bodies. He that loveth his wife loveth himself. For no man ever yet hated his own flesh; but nourisheth and cherisheth it, even as the Lord the church: For we are members of his body, of his flesh, and of his bones. For this cause shall a man leave his father and mother, and shall be joined unto his wife, and they two shall be one flesh.*

> *This is a great mystery: but I speak concerning Christ and the church. Nevertheless let every one of you in particular so love his wife even as himself; and the wife see that she reverence her husband." (Ephesians 5:22-33)"*

I told my two friends that God's ways are always better. When we honor the roles He gave the wife and husband, He blesses greatly our home, children, grandchildren and many others.

These two lovely people chose to follow the LORD and work out their differences God's way.

> *"For the word of God is quick, and powerful, and sharper than any twoedged sword, piercing even to the dividing asunder of soul and spirit, and of the joints and marrow, and is a discerner of the thoughts and intents of the heart." (Hebrews 4:12)*

God's Creation Ruined

> *"And when the woman saw that the tree was good for food, and that it was pleasant to the eyes, and a tree to be desired to make one wise, she took of the fruit thereof, and did eat, and gave also unto her husband with her; and he did eat. And the eyes of them both were opened, and they knew that they were naked; and they sewed fig leaves together, and made themselves aprons. . .*
>
> *Unto the woman he [God] said, I will greatly multiply thy sorrow and thy conception; in sorrow thou shalt bring forth children; and thy desire shall be to thy husband, and he shall rule over thee." (Genesis 3:6,7,16)*

Eve sinned first. I am persuaded she then seduced Adam to follow. God's creation was now ruined. Authority over God's creation was given to Adam. Was God's purposes for His creation, especially man, lost? NO!!! NO!!! NO!!! However, now that all mankind would be sinners, the cost to untold millions would be eternal separation from God. This is the cost, in the lives of others, for the sin Adam and Eve committed. There are always consequences for sin. Sin always hurts others, whether inside or outside your family.

For the LORD to complete His plan of redemption, He had to establish an order of authority (in the man) that would prevent Satan from destroying the family.

Overwhelmed with God's Holy Spirit

In 1987, I was visiting my communications office in Honolulu. I was in a rental car, driving parallel to the airport. I was already worshiping the LORD, when the song 'Majesty' came on the radio. This was the first time I heard 'Majesty'. As I was thanking the LORD for His goodness to me and my family, suddenly, I began to tear up and could not clearly see the road ahead. I pulled over to the shoulder and within a moment, God's Holy Spirit began to fill me with His presence, from the tips of my toes to the top of my head. God was allowing me to experience a very small part of His holiness. Soon, it felt like my entire body would explode. I knew that if the LORD did not stop, I would die. Strangely, I did not want the Holy Spirit to stop. However, I knew if He didn't, I would soon be dead. I cried out to God and said, 'LORD, if you don't stop, you are going to kill me.' Within a moment, I was back to normal.

To this day I do not know why the LORD allowed me to have this experience. What I do know is that He gave me a very revealing experience with His Holy presence.

I didn't think about this experience until about fifteen years later. Since then, I have not thought of it as an experience I should brag about.

Man Is God's Crowning Achievement

There is no creature in the whole universe more important to God than man. There is no greater value that God could have given men and women than to have made us in His own Holy image. Man is God's Crowning Achievement in all creation.

> "So God created man in his own image, in the image of God created he him; male and female created he them." (Genesis 1:27)

God's unsearchable love for man is why the Son of God (Jesus Christ) came to earth to restore our broken relationship with Him, which was necessary because of man's rebellion against God's holy commandments.

The Lord tells us:

> "For ALL have sinned, and come short of the glory of God." (Romans 3:23)

Man Is Created as Volitional Beings

When the LORD created man, He made us volitional beings. Each of us has the power to accept or reject God's Word. How could it be otherwise. God would never get pleasure from a robot who He pre-programmed to obey Him.

However, as volitional beings, the LORD is blessed when we willingly decide to follow His Word and leading. Because, we are created in the image of God, we can see the parallel between believers obeying the Word of God and the pleasure a Christian Dad gets when his son says, 'Yes Dad, I will do as you ask.'

It Shall Prosper in the Thing Whereto I Sent It

You and I cannot make anyone believe that they need a Savior. What we can do is share the truths we know about the Gospel and His Word. God will do the rest:

> "So shall my word be that goeth forth out of my mouth: it shall not return unto me void, but it shall accomplish that

> which I please, and it shall prosper in the thing whereto I sent it." (Isaiah 55:11)

Other Ways for Christians to Witness

Over the years, the LORD has provided many ways to share my faith with others, especially with children:

1. *Do You Know How to Shake Hands?*

   I would often reach out to shake the hand of our little ones at Church. I'd ask if they knew how to shake hands? The youngster (4 to 7 years old) would almost always try to shake my hand going up and down. However, I would force their hand to go left and right. Then I would say, 'no, no, no, I don't want that goofy stuff. This is the way to shake hands.' I would then move our hands up and down again.

   The next time we meet, I would ask if they remembered how to shake hands. They would say, 'Yes'. Again, I would shake their hands left to right and say, 'That's that goofy stuff.' Then I would move our hands up and down, and say, 'Now, that's the way to shake hands.' Years later, many of these little ones would remind me of the way I shook their hands.

2. *Fifteen Years Later*

   Recently, I walked into a restaurant and a young woman, maybe twenty-one years of age, was having dinner with her husband. She called my name and extended her hand to shake mine. I did not recognize her. She forced my shake to go left to right. I looked straight into her eyes, and I said, 'You remember.' She said 'Yes'. She was in my wife's Awana Girls Club at Church, fifteen years earlier. Joyce and her mother ministered to the little ones at our Church. I asked her name and after she told me, I recognized her mother first and then her. This experience gave me a wonderful opportunity to talk with her and her husband about their young marriage and how the LORD may want to use them in ministry.

After they left, I reached for the check and the server told me, 'The young couple paid for your meal.' Who would have thought?

3. *Twelve Years Later*

   Just a few days ago, two young men greeted me as I was composing and typing this book. One of them said, 'You don't remember me?' I said, 'No I don't, and I asked his name.' He said, 'Luke, when I was little you used to shake my hand from left to right. I still remember that.' I was stunned.

   I asked his age. He said, 'seventeen'. He remembered me from twelve years ago. Wow! And from a little handshake.

   It gave me an opportunity to have prayer with them and commit them both to the LORD.

4. *No Laughing, No Smiling, and No Having Fun*

   On Sunday mornings, I would occasionally stick my head into the children Sunday Schools Class. As the kids were preparing for class, I would say: 'Do you kids know Mr. Casper's rules?' They would look at me puzzled. Then I'd say, 'Mr. Casper's rules are: There's no laughing, no smiling and no having any fun.' Immediately they would break out in laughter.

   Over the years, many of these kids would remind me of my rules. Often, these moments of having fun with little ones, would give me opportunities to minister to them as teenagers and young adults.

5. *Do You Have Glue on Your Fingers?*

   Another silly custom I have with our Kids is to shake their hands and as we were about to separate our hands, hold their hand tighter and ask if they have glue on their fingers?

6. *My Sister's Statement*

   My Sister has been a Pastor's wife for about thirty-five years. A couple of years ago, she said to me: 'Did you know that because of your testimony in Christ, everyone in our family is saved?' I said, 'No, I never thought about it.' A few months later, she repeated the statement. Again, I said, 'No, 'I really never thought about it.'

   After a while, I became curious and decided to count the family members who, I had reason to believe, received Jesus as their Savior after I did. To my astonishment, the LORD, over the decades, has been working in the hearts of my family, and today there are forty-one members who are professing born again Christians. WOW!

7. *A Cousin Is Saved*

   A few weeks ago, my youngest brother asked me to call our cousin who was seven-years of age the last time I last saw her—about seventy-two years ago. He recently found where she lived and visited her in Texas. He also gave me her phone number.

   Over the years, I wondered if she became a Christian. When she answered her phone and found out who was calling, she was ecstatic with joy to hear from me (her two brothers and I grew up together).

   She is, in fact, a born-again believer, and a member of an evangelical church. Her granddaughter is getting married to a local pastor.

   Our God is so good! The joy I experienced while talking with my cousin was glorious. She did not want me to hang up, but before we did, I offered a prayer:

   > 'LORD Jesus, please don't let Satan steal Your best from my cousin or her family.'

All things, all things are possible with God!

8. *A Choking Man at a Restaurant*

   Bill Herman and I were eating lunch at a restaurant in Cuyahoga Falls, OH. Across the aisle from us, an old man was eating with, I believe, his granddaughter. Suddenly, the man started choking. He was gaging severely, and I knew something had to be done. No one was coming to help him. I immediately jumped up and grabbed the man, not knowing what I should do. I was thinking, maybe I should flip him upside down and force the clump of food out of his throat with gravity.

   At that point, another customer yelled: Do you know the Heimlich maneuver. I said 'No'. He said, 'Get behind him and place your fist below his chest and give a firm hard pull into his chest.' I did so, and the clump came out.

   The man started breathing again. His granddaughter thanked me profusely. I sat at his table for a moment and said to him, 'You know you were only moments from eternity.' I had the feeling his granddaughter was a born-again Christian, however, I did not share the Gospel with him. A decision I regret to this day.

9. *Youth Ministry to Topsail Island*

   On a youth ministry trip to Topsail Island, North Carolina, the leader of our group wanted me to teach the youth how they can witness for Christ.

   Our plan was to take eight youths with us and assign two of them to a motel room. The Youth Leader and I would have to share a double wide bed. Before we started on our nine-hour trip, the wife of our Youth Leader said to him, 'Now don't forget, no cuddling.' When we returned from the trip, his wife asked if we had a restful time. I told her, 'No, I slept with one eye open all week long.' We all had a good laugh.

While on the beach (carrying our Bibles) the group leader and I began walking toward four Marines who were enjoying the sun and surf. They were drinking beer as we approached them. One of the Marines saw us coming and kicked his beer can over. The other three did the same. Isn't it amazing how the Word of God brings conviction to even strong men.

We introduced ourselves and began talking with them about the Bible and the LORD. When we were done, all four of these Marines gave their hearts to Jesus. This was quite an object lesson for our youth.

By the time this five-day trip to the beach was over, the LORD gave us eight people who became Christians.

> 'Bless you LORD for allowing us to be part of your redemptive plan throughout the ages.'

10. *Leading a Stranger to Jesus at a Restaurant*

This morning, while enjoying breakfast, a young twenty-seven-year-old man, who was sitting next to me, asked what I do. I told him I was retired, but very active as an Evangelist and businessman. He told me, his sixty-eight-year-old father was also an Evangelist and would pass out tracts in parking lots.

We began to talk about the things that were important to him: science, biology, philosophy, comparative religions, and mathematics. It was obvious to me; he was not an average young man.

Gradually, he began asking me questions about his areas of interest. I reasoned with him for two and a half hours, after which I said, 'Brandon, are you ready to find God through faith in Jesus Christ?' He said, 'Yes'. I held his hand and told him, 'You must have a humble, honest heart and recognize that you are a sinner.' He said, 'Yes, I do.' At that point, I lead him through the sinner's prayer, and he was gloriously saved and became a member of the Family of God.

> *'Thank you, LORD, for my meeting with Brandon this morning. Bless you for allowing me to have such a glorious time reasoning with him and leading him to salvation in Jesus Christ. Please seal him with your Holy Spirit and lead him to a Bible preaching Church. AMEN!"*

SUMMARY

Over five decades, the LORD has sent me many men, women, and children who I have been privileged to lead to righteousness through Jesus Christ.

My friends, people everywhere need Jesus. We are the only ones who the LORD has commissioned to tell them how they can have a personal relationship with Jesus Christ. Sadly, there are not many Christians who are willing to share their faith with others. When we allow the LORD to use us, we grow in our own faith and learn how to trust in God's methods, provisions, and miracles.

Christians Are the Only People God Uses to Lead others to Jesus

Ask the LORD how you can be an effective minister/servant for Him. Search for His direction through prayer and in the Word of God. Maybe, He will lead you to become a Pastor, or a foreign Missionary, or an Evangelist, or Hospitality Host, or Choir Director, or a Sunday School teacher, or a trusted witness with others, or a Home Care Provider, or other Christian service, etc.

God also calls His Sons and Daughters to be Christian Scientists, Businessmen, Military Leaders, Doctors, Politicians, Lawyers, etc. There is a unique place in Christian service for each of us.

Seek Him while there is still time. Trust Him for the work He has given you. God has promised to direct your steps.

> ' *"For it is God which worketh in you both to will and do of His good pleasure." (Philippians 2:13)*

> "A man's heart deviseth his way: but the LORD directeth his steps." (Proverbs 16:9)
>
> " . . . I will never leave thee, nor forsake thee." (Hebrews 13:5)'

Christians Are the Most Powerful People on the Planet

> ' "Now then we are ambassadors for Christ, as though God did beseech you by us: we pray you in Christ's stead, be ye reconciled to God." (2 Corinthians 5:20)'

As Ambassadors for Christ, Christians are the most powerful people on the planet. When we tell someone about God's Word and the Gospel, the listener must do one of three things:

1. He can say 'I am not interested.'
2. He can say 'I'll think about it,' or
3. He can say 'Yes, I want to ask Jesus to be my Savior.'

Do not be intimidated when you are told: 'I am not interested', or 'I'll think about it.' Remember what the LORD tells us:

> "So shall My word be that goes forth from My mouth; It shall not return to Me void, But it shall accomplish what I please, And it shall prosper in the thing for which I sent it." (Isaiah 55:11)

God's Word will start working the moment someone hears it.

Persistence in Witnessing

In 1970, I worked for a Sales Manager who told his sales team that the common denominator for success is being able to do that which you don't want to do.

When a salesman tells a prospect about the benefits of his product, he does not expect to sell everyone he talks to. He might make a sale every fourth presentation.

The same principle is true when witnessing for Jesus. When you share the Gospel with others, maybe only one of four people will say:

> 'Yes, I want to ask Jesus to be my Savior.'

At this moment there is joy in heaven, and you will share in it.

I do not believe I have ever had a more satisfying experience than when someone has said to me: *'Yes, I want to ask Jesus to be my Savior.'*

Persevere in your walk and service for the LORD. Remember, with Him all things are possible.

> "Therefore, my beloved brethren, be ye stedfast, unmoveable, always abounding in the work of the Lord, forasmuch as ye know that your labour is not in vain in the Lord." (1 Corinthians 15:58)

> "For God so loved the world, that he gave his only begotten Son, that whosoever believeth in him should not perish, but have everlasting life. For God sent not his Son into the world to condemn the world; but that the world through him might be saved. He that believeth on him is not condemned: but he that believeth not is condemned already, because he hath not believed in the name of the only begotten Son of God. And this is the condemnation, that light is come into the world, and men loved darkness rather than light, because their deeds were evil. For every one that doeth evil hateth the light, neither cometh to the light, lest his deeds should be reproved. But he that doeth truth cometh to the light, that his deeds may be made manifest, that they are wrought in God." (John 3:16-21)

Chapter 9

Street Corner & Jail Ministries

In 1973, I was asked to be the Director of our Youth Ministry at Stow Alliance Fellowship. We had twenty young people (eighteen to twenty-one years of age) in our group. My burden was to teach them how to minister to others.

Becoming Chaplains at the County Jail

While preaching at downtown Akron, OH, I learned that one of the Vice Presidents of a local bank, across the street from where I was preaching, was the Chaplain at the Summit County Jail. While visiting with him, I asked if I would be allowed to have a Bible Study with the inmates. He was delighted, and after a security check made me a Chaplain.

The LORD was surely leading me into an exciting ministry that would eventually lead three hundred men to Jesus Christ, fifty of whom I baptized in the showers.

A Special Tribute to an Eighteen-Year-Old

There are three ranges (levels) in the jail that house inmates. During one of my early Bible Studies a young man, by the name of Steven, asked if it would be okay for him to bring other prisoners to the Study. I said, 'Absolutely'.

In short time, Steven began bringing prisoners to the Bible Study from other parts of the range—some of whom became Christians.

Steven was a Trustee and scheduled to be released soon. He was threatened by other prisoners who demanded that he bring drugs into the jail. As a Trustee, he was allowed to work outside the jail during the day. He was told, if he did not sneak drugs into the Jail, they would have prisoners at the State Prison, where his brother was an inmate, cause him great harm.

Steven was only eighteen years old at the time. Because of him, our Bible Study grew in numbers. In fact, I had to ask two brothers from Church if they would help me by teaching a Bible Study on two other ranges. They both agreed. Every week, we witnessed men coming to Jesus.

Steven eventually succumbed to the threats and brought drugs into the Jail. He was caught, and now he was facing many additional years in prison. One night, while he was in the dispensary, he decided to hang himself.

Oh, how I ache inside just telling this tragic story. Steven is home with the LORD now, but how Satan works to hurt God's people. Had Steven lived, we may have had many hundreds more giving their lives to Jesus.

> 'Oh JESUS, please don't allow even one of Steven's family, or extended family, die without being saved. AMEN'

Bible Study Lasts Five Years

Our Bible Study, on all three ranges, lasted five years. I counted three hundred men who gave their lives to Jesus Christ, fifty of whom I baptized in the showers. My Pastor, at the time, had misgivings about baptizing them in the showers. However, I had no baptismal facility in the jail, and I did not know if I would ever see them again. Also, I did not know when they would be released from incarceration.

I suspect there were other prisoners who gave their hearts to Jesus, and I may have missed them in my count.

Can Smoking Keep a Man from Going to Heaven

One evening, there were maybe twelve prisoners attending my Bible Study. One of the prisoners asked: 'Do you think smoking will keep a man from going to heaven?'

I followed up with a question: 'What would you do if I came into this range with a cigarette in my mouth, a can of beer in my left hand, and a Bible in my right hand,' and said, 'Come on fellas, let's have a Bible Study?' His reply was quick and forceful. 'I wouldn't come.' I asked 'why?' and he said, 'Because Reverends simply don't do that.'

I replied, 'Now you know why I don't smoke, nor drink alcohol. Others would be offended, and that would limit my ability to share my Christian testimony with them.'

As for your question: 'Will smoking prevent a man from going to heaven?', the answer is, 'No'. 'Jesus' blood covers every sin. If the man has confessed his sins and with a humble and honest heart asked the LORD to forgive him, then he will go to heaven. He immediately becomes a child of God and is adopted into the family of God.

> "For whosoever shall call upon the name of the Lord [Jesus Christ] shall be saved." (Romans 10:13)

Salvation, through Jesus Christ, is available to everyone: rich, poor, fat, skinny, smart, dumb, pretty, ugly, old, young, etc.

A beautiful example of the grace of God is the story of the thief on the Cross. The thief asked Jesus:

> *"And he said unto Jesus, Lord, remember me when thou comest into thy kingdom. . .. And Jesus said unto him, Verily I say unto thee, To day shalt thou be with me in paradise." (Luke 23:42,43)*

Jesus was only hours from His own death. There was no special anointing, no baptism, no laying on of hands, etc. for the thief. All the thief had to do was believe Jesus, that He is the Son of God and the redeemer of all mankind.

Salvation Is the First Step

Remember, your salvation is only the first step in God's plan for your life. He also wants you to grow in your knowledge and walk with Him, and He wants you to share your faith with others.

Keeping yourself from the practices of this world will allow you to share Jesus Christ with love, honesty and authority.

> "But grow in grace, and in the knowledge of our Lord and Saviour Jesus Christ. To him be glory both now and forever. Amen. (2 Peter 3:18)

My Youth Became Chaplains

As the Director of our youth at Church, I still did not know how to help them grow in the LORD without first putting them into a ministry. Then it occurred to me, maybe the Jail Chaplain would allow me to assign each prisoner, who was now a new Christian, to one of my youths for follow up and discipling.

I told the idea to the Chaplain, and he was most agreeable. In fact, he made each one of my youths, who wanted to participate in the jail ministry, an Assistant Chaplain with their own Badges.

We would assign one of our youths to meet weekly with a prisoner who had recently received Jesus Christ as his Savior. Our young people would minister to prisoners with prayer, answer questions, and read portions of the Bible to help him grow in the LORD.

This youth ministry proved to be a wonderful way to strengthen the faith of our youth and at the same time help prisoners know that there are young people who care for them.

Looking Back

Looking back to when I asked God not to allow me to see death until I have led 1,000 people to Jesus Christ, the Jail Ministry was an early step, that God used, on my journey to 90,000.

Needed Encouragement from a Special Saint of God

Twenty-five years after we first joined Stow Alliance Fellowship, my prayer partner and his wife visited with Joyce and me in North Carolina. He and his wife have since passed away. Again, these were two gems God sent my way to encourage us over the years.

He said to me, 'Ray, no one has accomplished, at Stow Alliance, what you have since our Church started nearly fifty years ago.' I was stunned and humbled.

While I was a member at Stow Alliance, it never occurred to me that my work was that noticeable. I had been concerned about growing in the LORD, sharing my testimony with others, honoring the LORD with my life, and bringing the unsaved to Jesus.

God has wonderful ways of confirming His pleasure with the work Christians do in the Church. However, at the time my brother told me this, I really needed his encouragement.

Street Ministry Begins in Akron, OH

While I was a student at Moody Bible Extension Studies, the LORD moved my heart to begin preaching on street corners. I began in downtown Akron, OH. I would set up speakers and a music stand on which I read the Word of God to the public. Sometimes, I would take my eldest son, six years of age. He would pass out tracts while I taught from the Bible. One day he said to me, 'Dad, every time you take me with you, I don't want to go and I'm afraid, but after we go, I always feel better and am glad we went.' AMEN!

Some experiences we had in Akron included: a passerby spitting on me while I was preaching, a priest scorning me as he walked by, some walking around me to avoid listening to my preaching, some people opening their office windows to listen, and an old lady placing a $1.00 bill on my music stand. I pray for that woman's family, till this day, that God would save every member of her immediate and extended family.

Other cities I preached in were Youngstown, OH, Canton, OH, Cleveland, OH and Tampa, FL.

Youngstown, OH—A Special Street Ministry Experience

In Youngstown, OH, I set up my speakers on a public sidewalk across from an open-air mall. About twelve people gathered around about showing interest in the Word of God. A woman started to yell at me from a second-floor window, demanding that I stop preaching. She said, 'I needed a permit to preach.' I yelled back at her, 'You don't need a permit to preach the Gospel' and kept on preaching. Apparently, she called the police because a young officer came up to me and asked if I had a permit. I told him you don't need a permit to preach the Gospel. He was polite but showed some authority in his question. The people who were standing around us started yelling at the officer, telling him to leave me alone, and that I was doing a good thing. The officer, feeling a bit threatened, told me he would go back to the precinct and find out if a permit was needed. He said he would return with the answer.

While he was away, it began to rain heavily. The twelve or so people around me left. I too picked up my equipment and left. I do not know the answer the officer was given at his precinct.

> 'Again, thank you LORD, for allowing me to be part of your ministry to prisoners, youth and others while at Stow Alliance Fellowship.'

Chapter 10

Restoring the Years

THE PHRASE "... RESTORE *to you the years that the locust hath eaten*" is a biblical metaphor that appears in the Book of Joel in the Old Testament. It symbolizes restoration, redemption, and God's promise to restore what has been lost or destroyed. It conveys hope and renewal.

> *"And I will restore to you the years that the locust hath eaten, the cankerworm, and the caterpillar, and the palmerworm, my great army which I sent among you. And ye shall eat in plenty, and be satisfied, and praise the name of the LORD your God, that hath dealt wondrously with you: and my people shall never be ashamed." (Joel 2:25-26)*

In essence, these scriptures emphasize God's grace, mercy, and the promise of restoration after a period of hardship or loss.

Providing for My Wife in Our Senior Years

Over the years, having suffered through so many calamities, I often wondered how I would provide for my wife and family when I was old. Most of the time we were broke because of business failures, ministry expenses, stock market crashes, medical expenses, etc.

I was deeply troubled, not knowing how I would care for my wife.

Five By-Pass Heart Surgery

On December 31, 2019, I became very ill. The Cardiologist ordered immediate heart surgery. My pulmonary system nearly stopped working. On January 3rd, 2020, I was in surgery having five heart bypasses. My recovery took ten months.

Before I went to surgery, I ordered the Gospel Letter be sent to fifty-four nations.

For the last four and a half years, I have not been able to work and produce income. Miraculously, the LORD through His unspeakable mercies and provisions, provided me with $100,000, just when I needed it.

One day, my sister called letting me know that she wanted me to receive my inheritance of $100,000 before she died. I said to my sister, whom I have always loved and respected, 'I'm about to fall off this chair.' I did not know anything about this inheritance. A few days later, I received her check for $100,000.

Our God Is Faithful

In early 2022, Joyce was diagnosed with an aggressive strain of Melanoma cancer. She began to get severely ill and spent most of the next one and a half years in hospitals, at Oncology Clinics, Xray and therapy facilities, and finally an extended care center for the terminally ill. Once again, our medical expenses began to increase, but this time, we had funds to pay them.

My Service-Connected Disabilities Become Blessings

During my tour of duty on the USS Borie DD 704, I was injured from a two-story fall onto a steel deck. I was also exposed to Asbestos which caused serious lung damage which I did not begin to feel the effects of until I was in Law School in 1969. On both occasions, I did not believe, as a young eighteen-year-old, I was seriously injured. When I asked the Medical Officer (who was preparing my Medical Discharge) if I could finish my tour, he granted my request.

The Veterans Administration decided in 2023 that I should receive disability pay, and started to send me monthly checks that are making up for the years of lost income that the canker worm had eaten.

Here, I am wondering how I will provide for my wife and myself when we are seniors, and the LORD had already worked it out. All I had to do was stay on course with the LORD and trust Him by faith.

> *"But without faith it is impossible to please him: for he that cometh to God must believe that he is, and that he is a rewarder of them that diligently seek him."* (Hebrews 11:6)

Chapter 11

Look Unto the Fields

Have you ever considered what the LORD meant when He said 'look on the fields . . . ':

> ". . . I say unto you, Lift up your eyes, and look on the fields; for they are white already to harvest. (John 4:35)

Can't you feel the LORD's heart when He said *'look on the the fields; for they are white already to harvest.?*

From eternity past, our Creator and Savior knew that He would have to go to a cruel, bloody Cross and suffer immeasurably so you and I can be pardoned from His Father's judgments for our sins. Imagine, Jesus knew (from eternity past) what pain and suffering He would bear in order to pardon you and me from the penalty of our sins. Why did He do this?

The answer is our God is a Holy, Righteous Creator, whose intention is to reclaim His creation back from Satan's evil devices and complete His original purposes for creating man. The LORD has always wanted to share His goodness with men, but now, the only way He would be able to do so, is to pardon us from our sin. He accomplished this by having His Son, Jesus Christ suffer in our place on a cruel Cross at Calvary.

My Son's Declaration

One day, my son said to me, 'Dad, I think you got those 1,000 souls.' I said, 'Son, I don't think so. I never counted them.' My Son repeated his statement and again, 'I said, Son, I don't know, I never counted them. But if I did, maybe it is time for Dad to go home.' He looked back at me and said, 'No Dad, that's not what I meant.'

Little did my Son know, but the LORD was using him to begin preparing me for the greatest harvest of souls in my lifetime.

One Billion Database Records

Over the last twenty-five years, I operated a marketing company that had many ups and downs. My hopes were that I would be able to generate enough income so our expenses for ministry, family, and initiatives would be met. Of course, this seldom happened.

Yes, there were times when we generated good income, but it didn't last. On three occasions the economy collapsed, and I was forced into bankruptcies.

However, over the last eight years, I was able to purchase large blocks of database records in one hundred and fifty-six nations. My first purchase was for 100 million records. My second purchase was 250 million. Then I was able to purchase 400 million. Eventually, I wound up with 1.8 billion database records in 156 nations.

I asked myself, why am I buying these records, and how should I use them? I had no equipment capable of processing and deploying them. Deploying them on the Internet was prohibited by a consortium of ISP's, who were trying to control traffic on the Internet.

In 2009, Congress passed a law allowing commercial and ministry use of the Internet. Suddenly, the LORD opened my eyes to how I would eventually lead 88,900 people to Jesus Christ:

> "And it shall come to pass in the last days, saith God, I will pour out of my Spirit upon all flesh: and your sons and your daughters shall prophesy, and your young men shall see visions, and your old men shall dream dreams:" (Acts 2:17)

It occurred to me that I should compose a Gospel Letter. The Internet would be the vehicle by which I would send the Gospel to people around the world. Through prayer and a great deal of labor, I managed to discover ways the Gospel Letter could be sent to one hundred and fifty-six nations.

In late 2018, a very special friend and I worked out a way to make the first deployment. We sent the Gospel Letter to twenty Muslim nations. On the first count, 1,900 people received Christ as their Savior. Admittedly, we were learning and made many mistakes. However, over the next year, we began to realize that the LORD had provided us with one of the most inexpensive and effective ways for the Church to reach unreached peoples in one hundred and fifty six nations.

In 2019, I prepared a deployment of the Gospel Letter to fifty-four nations. It would include a cover letter, with an explanation as to why man is God's crowning achievement in all creation. The first three paragraphs read:

> "There is no creature in the whole universe more important to God than man. Man is God's crowning achievement in all creation. Why do you ask?...Because we are made in His image. There is no greater value that God could have given men and women than to have made us in His own holy image.
>
> God's unsearchable love for man is why the Son of God (Jesus Christ) came to earth to restore our

broken relationship with Him, which was caused by man's rebellion against God's holy righteousness and commandments."

The Lord tells us:

> "For ALL have sinned, and come
> short of the glory of God."
> (Romans 3:23)

This means you, me and the rest of mankind.

Second Gospel Letter

Our Gospel Letter to fifty-four nations included a link to a digital Study Bible for the Old and New Testaments. The Bible can be read in 80+ different languages. It includes Strong's Concordance, commentaries, Greek and Hebrew texts, parallel sermons, audios, visuals, Interlinear, Lexicon, and more. It can be accessed on computers, cell phones, tabloids, and wristwatches.

Most importantly, our Gospel Letter does not wait for someone to find us. People around the world receive it in their homes, at work, at play, while vacationing, even while traveling.

We also included a link to a two-hour Jesus Film. It can be viewed and heard in 1,749 languages.

Challenging the Reader to Make a Decision to Become a Child of God

The following four steps are in the Gospel Letter, and explain how people receive Jesus Christ as their Savior:

> To receive God's gift of love all you have to do is 'accept it'. You do not have to pay anything for it. With an humble, honest and repentant heart say the following prayer:

1. I believe Jesus Christ paid the penalty for my sins when He was crucified on a Cross at Calvary
2. I believe Jesus Christ died, was buried and rose from the dead on the 3rd day and ascended into heaven
3. Lord, please forgive me of my sins and send your Holy Spirit into my heart to seal me and to guide me as your child and follower of your Son Jesus Christ
4. Thank you Lord for hearing my prayer, forgiving me of my sins and making me a child of God.

CONGRATULATIONS! By saying this prayer, you became a 'born again' Christian and member of God's family. God's Holy Spirit will now comfort and teach you about your new faith and walk in the Lord Jesus Christ. It is important that you begin reading the Bible regularly (God's inspired WORD that reveals Himself to man). We have provided special links below that allow you to study the Bible on-line in many different languages. God's Holy Spirit will reveal many wonderful things about God's plan for your life."

Let us know that you have made this exciting life changing decision. Confirm your decision by clicking this link:

<u>YES, I DID PRAY THIS PRAYER
TO BECOME A CHRISTIAN</u>

We will forward to you important information about your new faith in Jesus Christ that will help you grow in your Christian walk with the Lord (prayer, baptism, communion, family, prophecy, doctrine, and much more).

You will also be able to make comments and ask questions about the Bible (WORD of God) and related subjects.

> '*LORD JESUS, you have been awfully. good to the 'Kacprowicz' Casper family.*'

If you have interest in helping Ministry Channels, International send this Gospel Letter to one hundred and fifty six nations (one billion people representing upwards of 60% of the world's families) go to https://ministrychannels.org.

You can also contact me at (828) 385 2438 and director@ministrychannels.org.

Chapter 12

The Harvest and Blessings

IN LATE DECEMBER 2019, not knowing that in a few days I would be sent to the hospital as an emergency heart surgery patient, I had released 100 million Gospel Letter to 54 nations.

As I was recovering, I tried to count the number of people who clicked this link:

<u>YES, I DID PRAY THIS PRAYER
TO BECOME A CHRISTIAN</u>

Because I was limited to the amount of data I could download from hospital servers, I was not able to accurately collect all 'New Christian' responses until I was released from the hospital.

As the weeks passed by, I was able, while at the hospital, count most of the confirmations from 'New Christians' in 54 nations. They came in slowly. At first a few hundred, then a few thousand, and finally we received 350,000 clicks saying they prayed the prayer to become a Christian (There were thousands more who clicked the links to download our digital Study Bible and Jesus Film.)

Knowing a little about database construction, and how techies use bots to damage responses, I decided to take a more careful count of the 350,000 responses.

The first thing I did was remove duplicates. Then, I removed the autoresponders. I took out all emails that did not come from an individual. When I was finished there were 70,000 individuals who said they received Jesus Christ as their Savior.

Joyce Develops Melanoma Cancer

Shortly after my recovery, Joyce developed two types of cancer. Just about all my time was spent as her primary care giver. She was on two chemo treatments a day. Her body was so weak that she developed pneumonia. We barely got her to the hospital in time. She was put in Intensive Care for ten days, during which she was semi-conscious.

I stayed with Joyce day and night. She could not communicate with me.

During these ten days, a thought kept running through my head: 'You didn't have 70,000 decisions for Christ. Your assumptions were wrong. Your extrapolations were wrong. Your conclusions were wrong. For three days, while staying with Joyce, these thoughts kept going through my mind.

Finally, I decided to go through the 350,000 again, to confirm a correct count. It took me three more days, but when I was finished, I didn't have 70,000 decisions for Jesus—I had 87,000, plus, the 1,900 in Muslim countries. There may have been many more who I removed from the count because I could not identify them as individuals (e.g. info@; support@; director@; auto-responders; bots; and so on).

When I summed it all up, while my wife was dying in Intensive Care, the LORD confirmed that He gave Joyce and me, not 1,000 souls who I asked for fifty-three years earlier, but 88,900, plus upwards of 1,000 who were lead to the LORD one on one. Oh LORD Jesus, you are so wonderful. AMEN! WOW!

> "Now unto him that is able to do exceeding abundantly above all that we ask or think, according to the power that worketh in us," (Ephesians 3:20)

Beyond Measure Thankful, But Not Satisfied

As I reflected on what the LORD was confirming to me, I told Him that I am beyond measure thankful that He allowed me to have such a ministry. I praised Him with worship and thanksgiving.

Then I said, 'Lord as grateful as I am for what you have done, I am not satisfied. 'You have also given me a database of one billion people in one hundred and fifty-six nations. I now know how to reach these people with the Gospel. Would you please lead me, so I can share the Gospel with them as well.'

PRAISE THE LORD! BLESS YOU LORD!

THANK YOU, LORD, FOR YOUR KINDNESS
TO ME AND MY FAMILY!

*Please keep me from failing you or disgracing
you during the days I have left.*

Chapter 13

Are Christians Pacifists?

ONE SUNDAY MORNING, I told my Sunday School Class about the experience I had in Youngstown, OH. There was a new student in the class, and he took exception to how I responded to the woman in a second-floor window and the police officer who told me that I needed a permit to preach the Gospel. I told them both that you don't need a permit to preach the Word of God, or the Gospel.

This visitor demanded that I show him where in the Bible it says I can disobey the laws of man. I took him to several passages in the Old Testament that he rejected. He said, 'Show me a verse in the New Testament.' I showed him some verses in the New Testament (some are quoted in this book), and he rejected them.

I asked him if he was married. He said divorced. Do you have any children, he said, 'Three sons.' I said to him, 'Assume for a minute an assailant comes flying into this room, grabs your youngest son and begins beating him severely. What would you do?' He did not think about it for very long. He said, 'I would do nothing.' I asked if he would start praying? He said, 'Yes.'

This denial of what the LORD tells us in Scriptures requires a commonsense response.

> "If it be possible, as much as lieth in you, live peaceably with all men." (Romans 12:18)

> "And he said unto them, When I sent you without purse, and scrip, and shoes, lacked ye any thing? And they said, Nothing. Then said he unto them, But now, he that hath a purse, let him take it, and likewise his scrip: and he that hath no sword, let him sell his garment, and buy one. For I say unto you, that this that is written must yet be accomplished in me, And he was reckoned among the transgressors: for the things concerning me have an end. And they said, Lord, behold, here are two swords. And he said unto them, It is enough. (Luke 22:35-38)

At the time this stranger came to my class, Joyce had died ten days before. He later apologized to me for his timing. He also quickly found another Church to attend.

> "For I say unto you, that this that is written must yet be accomplished in me," (Luke 22:37)

I am persuaded that the above verse means after Jesus ascended into heaven, and the Church is created, there will be violence on the earth to prevent the Gospel from being propagated to the nations.

The sword (physical weapon) will be needed to prevent our extinction. The Sword (Word of God) is for penetrating the darkness. Trusting the LORD by faith for the wisdom to know when to use them is imperative.

These Scriptures, and others, tell us that if it is impossible to live peaceably with others, then we are required to respond with force (the sword represents the force).

Jesus was telling His disciples that Israel had rejected Him as their Messiah and King (as their king He would have provided them with protection and necessities as He did the first time He sent them into villages.) (Luke 22:35-38)

> "When Pilate saw that he could prevail nothing, but that rather a tumult was made, he took water, and washed his hands before the multitude, saying, I am innocent of the blood of this just person: see ye to it. Then answered all the people, and said, His blood be on us, and on our children. Then released he Barabbas unto them: and when he had scourged Jesus, he delivered him to be crucified." (Matthew 27:24-26)

Now God's plan to evangelize the gentiles would have to go forward without Israel leading the way.

> "I the LORD have called thee in righteousness, and will hold thine hand, and will keep thee, and give thee for a covenant of the people, for a light of the Gentiles;" (Isaiah 42:6)

The LORD knew, in order for Him to bring salvation to the world (a commission that the Jews rejected), He would have to commission the Church composed of believers from all nations. Many of the Mosaic Laws of Israel, under the Kingdom Age, would not apply in the Church Age (a new dispensation), and consequently there would be a need for self-defense—represented by a sword.

> "Let every soul be subject unto the higher powers. For there is no power but of God: the powers that be are ordained of God. Whosoever therefore resisteth the power, resisteth the ordinance of God: and they that resist shall receive to themselves damnation. For rulers are not a terror to good works, but to the evil." (Hebrews 13:1-4)

> "Whoso sheddeth man's blood, by man shall his blood be shed: for in the image of God made he man." (Genesis 9:6)

God clearly says government is a terror to 'evil', not 'good'. So how are Christians to understand these verses when the government has caused the murder of upwards of eighty million Unborn Children in fifty-one years? The answer is in Romans 12:18 and Luke 22:35-38)

What Is the Christian's Duty When Government Rejects the Laws Governing God's Church

The LORD called me to be an Evangelist in the middle of the greatest destruction of human life in history. Over fifty-three years, He directed me to raise a banner and oppose the evil against our Unborn Children, our Constitutional Republic, and our Christian heritage. To accomplish this, He gave me the following Initiatives and Ministry:

1. The Article 5 Unborn Child Amendment (presented to Congress and two hundred plus Churches)
2. The Article 5 Countermand Amendment (presented to Congress and fifty State Legislatures)
3. Ministry Channels International (Worldwide Evangelistic Ministry)

Before Roe v Wade, starting in 1958, I was in the fight for America's survival while serving in the United States Navy. The Cold War was raging in China, Russia, South and Central America, and Southeast Asia.

These years were very tough for Joyce and me. Yes, we suffered many personal losses, but what hurt the worst were pacifistic teachings from my brethren.

The LORD was teaching me that I must not be silenced by doctrines that leave an open door for Satan and his emissaries to destroy America's Christian heritage and our Unborn Children.

> *"I have set watchmen on your walls, O Jerusalem; They shall never hold their peace day or night. You who make mention of the LORD, do not keep silent,"* (Isaiah 62:6)

I am persuaded that America is not just another country. In God's foreknowledge, He purposed America to propagate the Gospel and the Word of God to all nations. There are untold millions, in nearly every nation, who have been saved because of the missionary zeal of America's Christians.

The Christians' duty is to protect America's righteous laws and reject and change unrighteous ones.

Tools that God Has Provided for Ministry and Initiatives

Because of the deep conviction on my heart for the minds, souls and lives of men, I was forced to advance the greater part of the LORD's ministries and initiatives outside the organized Church.

Never in the history of the Church has the LORD provided such tools that can reach hundreds of millions of people, all over the world, with the Gospel of Jesus Christ:

1. worldwide Internet,
2. enormous collections of database records in over 156 nations, and
3. technical capabilities for deploying millions of Gospel messages in short periods of time.
4. a cost that is a fraction of other evangelical ministries

If the American Church continues to believe the devil's lie that she must keep out of:

1. aggressive evangelism (today only 5% of Christians will lead only one person to the Lord in their lifetime),
2. politics, and
3. government,

then there will be untold millions who will die a Christless eternity. There will also be tens of millions more Unborn Children who will die in the womb.

Our battle is to fight evil doctrines, such as abortion, with every righteous tool and authority the LORD has given Christians (especially in America), while at the same time sharing the Gospel with as many as possible.

> *"Watch ye, stand fast in the faith, quit you like men, be strong."* (1 Corinthian 16:13)

Are Christians Actively Sharing their Faith?

Several years ago, a Baptist denomination sponsored a survey of Christians asking if they ever led anyone to Jesus. Here's what they found:

1. 95% of Christians never lead anyone to salvation through Jesus Christ in their lifetime.
2. Only 5% of Christians will lead one person to the LORD in their lifetime.
3. Conclusion, 95% percent of Christians are clueless regarding the price Jesus Christ had to pay for their souls. They do not understand the Great Commission and its importance to God and men.
4. The Church is doing a terrible job bringing in the sheaves.

Some Church leaders caused me great anguish when they suggested that I focus on winning souls, and not get involved with politics or social issues (both are righteous issues). Most often these men were not actively winning souls themselves. There was almost no burden for the life of the Unborn Child (3,000 being murdered every day since 1973). Each child represents God's heritage, the father's heritage, and America's heritage.

There were none who joined with me in the Church, (except one) to advance the Unborn Child Amendment, or restore our Constitutional Republic, and Christian heritage.

Serving the LORD in the Church, Politics and Society

The LORD directed Joyce and me to continue sharing our faith with others, and at the same time, advance the Unborn Child Amendment and Countermand Amendment.

Jesus tells us that He came to seek and to save that which is lost. In Matthew 6:33, we are told it is our duty to actively seek the souls of men who Christ died for and are to be part of His Kingdom. At the same time, we should be actively installing, protecting, and obeying God's righteous laws in America.

Christians Must Not Abdicate Their Authority to Pacifists

We are not to abandon America by appeasing those who say the Church needs to stay out of politics and social issues.

The Founders were Christians, and every part of their work was political. They endeavored to codify righteous principles in every document. Future generations of Christians would have the duty to enforce the Biblical principles and laws written in the Constitution. The Founders went so far as to join the revolution that defied the established English Monarchy ruling in America.

Christians are the salt that the world needs to bring men under conviction for their wicked ways. I am persuaded that this means Christians are not to be pacifists, especially in America, where our government is founded on the truths from the Bible, and our representatives are elected by the people. The people, in our democratic Republic, have a grave duty to be informed of the affairs of government and protect God's righteous laws, especially, the sacred heritage the LORD has in Unborn Children.

> "And if it seem evil unto you to serve the LORD, choose you this day whom ye will serve; whether the gods which your fathers served that were on the other side of the flood, or the gods of the Amorites, in whose land ye dwell: but as for me and my house, we will serve the LORD." (Joshua 24:15)

Joshua challenged the people to make a choice between the gods which were before the flood, or the gods of the Amorites, or the LORD. God gave Israel a choice that they would be accountable for.

> "... Our Father which art in heaven, Hallowed be thy name. Thy kingdom come. Thy will be done in earth, as it is heaven." (Matthew 6:9,10)

In Matthew 6:9,10 and Proverbs 16:12 the LORD tells us that His righteous laws in heaven will be 'done on earth', not just in eternity, but on earth in today's world. They have to be defended and fought for, for future generations.

> "It is an abomination to kings to commit wickedness: for the throne is established by righteousness." (Proverbs 16:12)

In Proverbs 16:12 we are told the thrones of governments (on earth) are established by righteousness. Surely this means that God's people are to protect, install and obey the righteous laws of God, especially in America.

How, with these verses clearly telling us that the LORD wants His righteous laws established on earth, do we continue to avoid politics and government? Why has the Church become a doormat for Satan's emissaries by advocating pacifism?

> "Therefore to him that knoweth to do good, and doeth it not, to him it is sin." (James 4:17)

> If thou faint in the day of adversity, thy strength is small. If thou forbear to deliver them that are drawn unto death, and those that are ready to be slain; If thou sayest, Behold, we knew it not; doth not he that pondereth the heart consider it? and he that keepeth thy soul, doth not he know it? and shall not he render to every man according to his works? (Proverbs 24:10-12)

Chapter 14

Unborn Child Amendment

America's Light to the Nations Has Been Nearly Extinguished

When hearing the nightly news on January 22, 1973, that the United States Supreme Court decided to empower American mothers to abort their Unborn Children, on a whim, and with impunity, I was compelled to find a way to stop this coming infanticide. I also knew that America was now going to see the wrath of God as never before imaginable.

Fatalism

Fatalism is a philosophical doctrine that asserts events are predetermined and therefore inevitable. According to this belief, men are powerless to change the course of events.

There are many in the Church who make the following statement:

> 'God is in control, don't worry about it.'

Personally, I regard this statement, about the role of God, in the affairs of men, as the cause of God's people withdrawing from the battlefield and surrendering to Satan and his emissaries.

'God is in control, don't worry about it.' is fatalism. It is used to excuse men of their sins of omission and their duty before God to use 'free will' to protect and advance the purposes of God in our personal and national lives. In America, we are now eighty million babies too late because leaders in the Church taught this doctrinal error.

The phrase 'God's in Control' is correctly understood by recognizing God's foreknowledge. He knows what decisions free agent men and angels will make and the consequences that will result. He maintains control of His creation through the free will choices of men and angels. How, He is able to accomplish this is beyond me.

Without volition, there is no accountability on the part of men. Without volition we are mere robots bringing no fellowship or joy to our LORD.

These doctrines of fatalism and pacificism in America has neutered the Church and prevented her from aggressively pursuing the purposes of God.

> "I am the vine, ye are the branches: He that abideth in me, and I in him, the same bringeth forth much fruit: for without me ye can do nothing." (John 15:5)

When men seek the will of God and His purposes, the LORD begins to work on their behalf. For example, when we witness for the LORD, our responsibility to share His Gospel is accomplished. This is a volitional act and is required in order for others to learn of the love God has for them.

> "For with the heart one believes unto righteousness, and with the mouth confession is made unto salvation. (Romans 10:10)

The conversion of souls is in God's hands. Men have nothing to do with the work of salvation in the hearts of men.

Even the act of receiving Christ as our Savior requires a volitional decision by men before they get saved. Yes, God is leading them to repentance, but He still requires a volitional decision for accountability.

In a similar way, when men decide to seek a vision God has given them (such as finding ways to stop the slaughter of the Unborn, or protecting America's Constitutional Republic, or our Christian heritage), they make volitional decisions, and the LORD shows them how, by faith, to go forward.

Christian men are not to be pacifists! The LORD did not create men to be models of heathen fatalism. He looks for men to willingly seek Him and serve Him and engage the evil in their generation.

America is a very unique nation. The LORD gave our Founders the wisdom to establish Biblical truths and how to codify them in the Articles of Confederation, Declaration of Independence, Bill of Rights, and Constitution. I am persuaded, He also gave Christians Article 5 to protect our Christian heritage and to enforce righteousness in the future.

> "Be strong and of a good courage: for unto this people shalt thou divide for an inheritance the land, which I sware unto their fathers to give them." (Joshua 1:6)

Instead of engaging the battle and defending God's revealed truths, Christians have withdrawn and surrendered America to God's enemies.

> "And Moses besought the LORD his God, and said, LORD, why doth thy wrath wax hot against thy people, which thou hast brought forth out of the land of Egypt with great power, and with a mighty hand? . . . And the LORD repented of the evil which he thought to do unto his people. (Exodus 32:11,14)

The scriptures have many verses admonishing men to be strong and fight battles with the LORD. The scriptures tell us that the Lord is willing to change His mind when men repent and seek His forgiveness for their evil. This is not fatalism.

Israel Had Been Worshiping Idols

Israel had been worshiping idols and practicing the religions of the heathen round about them. God's compassion and willingness to relent from judgments He declared against His people can occur when men confess their sins and seek His forgiveness and leadership.

King Hezekiah's and Israel's future were not predetermined by the LORD. Yes, the LORD knew, in His foreknowledge, what Hezekiah's prayer would be, but He required Hezekiah to exercise 'free will' for accountability. Without free will, we are simply robots.

> "Did Hezekiah king of Judah and all Judah put him at all to death? did he not fear the LORD, and besought the LORD, and the LORD repented him of the evil which he had pronounced against them? Thus might we procure great evil against our souls." (Jeremiah 26:19)

After the People of Nineveh Repented

> "And God saw their works, that they turned from their evil way; and God repented of the evil, that he had said that he would do unto them; and he did it not." (Jonah 3:10)

After the people of Nineveh repented, God relented from the judgments He had declared against them. It demonstrates God's willingness to change His course based on human actions. There is no fatalism with God!

Jeremiah 18:8 shows God's desire to lead men to repentance and transformation.

Amos 7:3, 7:6 show God can change His mind when men earnestly seek His face and acknowledge His sovereignty.

Proposed Unborn Child Amendment

ARTICLE V
UNBORN CHILD AMENDMENT
ARTICLE 28
(or alternate number to be assigned by Congress)

Section 1. The Unborn offspring of human beings are persons from the time of conception and continually thereafter throughout their subsequent development: No Unborn person shall be intentionally deprived of life, or limb, or shall be subjected to intentionally inflicted harm.

Section 2. To secure the rights of Unborn persons, induced abortion is hereby prohibited within the United States which shall include the Several States, the District of Columbia, the Commonwealth of Puerto Rico, the Commonwealth of the Northern Mariana Islands and the territories and possessions of the United States.

Section 3. Congress shall have the power to enforce by appropriate legislation, the provisions of the Article.

Our Greatest Sin is America Rejecting God's Warnings to the Church and State Legislatures

Roe v. Wade, in 1973, was the evilest decision the United States Supreme Court ever made. With the stroke of a pen, it condemned eighty million babies to death, who were made in the image of God and for the purposes of God.

> "So God created man in his own image, in the image of God created he him; male and female created he them." (Genesis 1:27)

Every Aborted Child Represents God's Heritage

Every aborted child represents the destruction of God's heritage. The LORD has been completing His plan of redemption, through procreation, for 6,000 years.

There are approximately 3,700,000 live births in America each year, and approximately one million aborted Babies. From each one million abortions, if they had been allowed to live, there would be upwards of 400,000 people who would have become born-again believers. This is the heritage that God lost and will never enjoy. God intended that procreation and new births would continue endlessly into the future.

God purposed to populate the earth and heaven through procreation at the same time. No woman, no man, no government has been given the right to destroy the LORD's heritage by extinguishing it forever.

> "There is a way that seems right to a man, But its end is the way of death." (Proverbs 16:25)

> "'Listen to Me, O islands, and pay attention, you peoples from afar. The Lord called Me from the womb; from the body of My mother He named Me." (Isaiah 49:1)

> "If thou sayest, Behold, we knew it not; doth not he that pondereth the heart consider it? and he that keepeth thy soul, doth not he know it? and shall not he render to every man according to his works?" (Proverb 24:12)

The Good Samaritan

> "And Jesus answering said, A certain man went down from Jerusalem to Jericho, and fell among thieves, which stripped him of his raiment, and wounded him, and departed, leaving him half dead. And by chance there came down a

> *certain priest that way: and when he saw him, he passed by on the other side. And likewise a Levite, when he was at the place, came and looked on him, and passed by on the other side. But a certain Samaritan, as he journeyed, came where he was: and when he saw him, he had compassion on him, And went to him, and bound up his wounds, pouring in oil and wine, and set him on his own beast, and brought him to an inn, and took care of him. And on the morrow when he departed, he took out two pence, and gave them to the host, and said unto him, Take care of him; and whatsoever thou spendest more, when I come again, I will repay thee. Which now of these three, thinkest thou, was neighbour unto him that fell among the thieves? And he said, He that shewed mercy on him. Then said Jesus unto him, Go, and do thou likewise." (Luke 10:30-37)*

The wounded man on the road needed help. An half-Jewish, half-Gentile Samaritan had compassion and assisted the wounded man with money, housing, personal care, and transportation. Today, our religious leaders walk by abortion chambers (where 3,000 continue to be murdered daily) and do little or nothing to stop it:

> *"Surely this happened to Judah at the LORD's command, to remove them from His presence because of the sins of Manasseh and all that he had done, and also because of the innocent blood that he had shed; for he had filled Jerusalem with innocent blood, which the LORD would not pardon." (2 Kings 24:3,4)*

> *"And he made his son pass through the fire, and observed times, and used enchantments, and dealt with familiar spirits and wizards: he wrought much wickedness in the sight of the LORD, to provoke him to anger." (2 Kings 21:6)*

The Church has the blood of many of these aborted babies on her hands, especially when we remember that American Christians had the constitutional authority to stop this slaughter before it started.

I ache inside knowing that Joyce's and my fifty-one-year battle for the lives of eighty million Unborn Babies has failed.

Will weeping and confessions from the Church be enough for God to forgive us of this evil insanity and restore America's Christian heritage?

Caught Betwixt Two

My Evangelical ministry has been the greatest burden on my heart. At the same time, I felt a deep accountability to the LORD to find a way to stop the slaughter of His heritage. God often reminded me of His word:

> "But seek ye first the kingdom of God, and his righteousness; and all these things shall be added unto you." (Matthew 6:33)

Why the Need for an Article 5 Amendment?

Catholics organized the first Crisis Pregnancy Center, about fifteen years after Roe v. Wade was decided. During those fifteen years, I found myself compelled to try and persuade Christian leaders of the need to pass an Amendment that would permanently stop abortion in America. Over the years, I drove across country, from North Carolina, to Florida, to the Mid-West, and to California (sleeping in my car), trying to introduce the Unborn Child Amendment to Pastors. No one found the time to see me.

Work in Congress

While I was trying to find support among Churches, Joyce and I we're also working with Congress looking for sponsors to send the Amendment to State Legislatures for ratification, or to convene the Article 5 Amendment Convention (the first step in the Single-Issue Amendment ratification process). An Amendment can be created by Congress or State Legislatures calling for Legislatures or Conventions to ratify it. This is the Single-Issue

Amendment process that Congress used to ratify the Bill of Rights through State Legislatures.

When I visited Congress, I made it a point to kneel on the steps of Congress praying for the LORD to stop this unspeakable evil.

I found no support for the Unborn Child Amendment in the House of Representatives. However, there were two members of the Senate who were willing to help me, Senator Jessie Helms of North Carolina and Senator Strom Thurmond from South Carolina. I failed to enlist the support of anyone else.

There was literally no prospect for support by two thirds of Congress needed to send the Amendment to the State Legislatures for ratification, nor calling for an Article V Unborn Child Amendment Convention.

Pregnancy Centers should be Tax Exempt

This foolish notion gave no thought to the appointed duty the LORD has given all Christians to protect His heritage. [Tax Exempt status gives the Federal Government, through the Internal Revenue Service, authority to establish rules for Pregnancy Centers that would determine how Pro-Life Americans can fight for and protect human life.]

> "Blessed is the nation whose God is the LORD, and the people whom He hath chosen for His own inheritance." (Psalm 33:12)

When I was asked to be a Director for a Pregnancy Center in North Carolina, I declined on the grounds that I would not allow the IRS to limit how I should fight for the life of the Unborn Child. However, I do support this Pregnancy Center because they are saving souls and babies one at a time.

DEFENDERS OF THE UNBORN, WINNERS OF SOULS, CHRISTIAN PATRIOTS

Working with Churches

Joyce and I tried to convince the Church to join in the battle for the life of the Unborn Child. Since 1973, feminists organized the body politic to protect their 'so called right to privacy'. They demanded that their body is theirs to do with as they please, and the Unborn Child was only a piece of tissue that was expendable at their whim. This Satanic falsehood eventually became the moral compass of at least 50% of American adult women. It crept into the Church like wildfire.

1. Joyce arranged for me a phone meeting with the Pastor of a large Evangelical Church. After I introduced myself, the Pastor said, 'You're not going to recruit me to join your initiative.'

2. Joyce set an appointment for me with another Pastor who agreed to talk with me before I would be allowed to speak in his pulpit on behalf of the Unborn Child Amendment. As I recall, I had to drive a great distance to keep this meeting. When I met with the Pastor, 'He said his pulpit is used only for preaching the Gospel.' I asked him, 'How many souls have you turned to the LORD?' He remained silent. I told him, 'The LORD has given me many hundreds of men who I led to Jesus. Is that not enough to qualify me to speak in your pulpit on behalf of the Unborn Child Amendment?' The Pastor never invited me to talk to his congregation.

3. A small independent church in Kentucky invited me to speak in their pulpit on behalf of the Unborn Child. I had a V8 Chevy which guzzled gas like crazy. After the Church service, the Pastor invited me to have dinner with him and members of his Church at the local steak house. They did not take a love offering. I had $20 in my pocket, with about a half a tank of gas. To get home, I had to drive 9 hours. I prayed the entire way home that the LORD would stretch my gas mileage. Miraculously, the LORD guided me home safely.

4. The Pastor who blessed my heart beyond measure was in Pennington Gap, VA. He scheduled me to speak to his

250-member congregation on behalf of the Unborn Child. We first met with him and his Elders in his Pastoral Office. One of his Elders walked up to me and said, 'He would be honored if I would sign his Bible.' I was overwhelmed and greatly humbled. After prayer, we entered the sanctuary. The Church was packed wall to wall. Maybe 450 people were ready to listen to how we can amend the Constitution with the Unborn Child Amendment. The Pastor called on the people to sign my petition to Congress. I think all of them signed it. The Church gave me a very substantial donation. After leaving, about two weeks later, I received a large box with 5,000 signed petitions to Congress. The Pastor told his people to go out into the highways and hedges and compel them to sign my petition. Along with the petitions, was another substantial donation that melted my heart.

> *LORD JESUS, bless you for sending me this Godfearing man who labored hard on behalf of your heritage. Please bless him, his immediate and extended family, his Church and ministries GREATLY! AMEN!*

5. Joyce scheduled me for a presentation at an Evangelical Church in Central North Carolina. The Pastor shared my resume with the congregation and said, 'I don't know how this man did what he has done on behalf of souls and the Unborn.' After the presentation, an American History teacher told him that I was correct on every point of Constitutional history and law. A young woman said, 'She had heard my presentation at another Church, and because of it, she did not go forward with the abortion she had scheduled.

LORD JESUS, I LOVE YOU GREATLY!

Over many years, the LORD allowed me to speak at 200+ Churches. A few allowed me to speak on Sunday morning for short segments. Other presentations were scheduled for Tuesday, Wednesday, and Sunday nights. Most of these Churches were great distances from my home.

Regrettably, I was not able to muster, from the Churches, the collective support needed for Congress.

Fighting for our Constitutional Republic, the Unborn Child, and the souls of men were not priorities for the Church.

Chapter 15

Countermand Amendment

OVER THE YEARS THERE have been patriots, across the country, who were following my work with the Article V Unborn Child Amendment. They asked me to sponsor and direct a Single-Issue Amendment that would curb Federal government excesses. At first, I was not interested because all my attention was focused on Ministries and the Unborn Child Amendment. Because the interest from the Church was poor, I finally agreed thinking that such a States Rights Amendment might preserve our Constitutional Republic, Christian heritage and restrict abortions.

The burden on my heart, for the souls of men, did not diminish because I was to be the Executive Director of the Article V Countermand Amendment. Nor did my anguish and work to stop the slaughter of the Unborn Child change. The LORD required of me to serve Him in all three ministries and at the same time.

State Legislators' Round Table

We established the *State Legislators' Round Table*, an Internet Radio call-in forum for State Legislators from across the country.

Legislators would participate in a nationwide discussion on how Article 5 can be used and learn what the Article V Countermand Amendment can do to preserve our Constitutional Republic.

An Enormous Undertaking

The undertaking to amend the United States Constitution, with a Single-Issue Countermand Amendment, I knew would be enormous. Here, I am seventy-four years of age, thinking it was time for my wife and me to rest for our remaining years. And yet, I knew America was a country God chiseled out of the peoples of the world with a purpose that was not yet complete (otherwise, we would not still exist as the wealthiest, most powerful nation the world has ever known).

America's Christian heritage was foremost in my mind that triggered my conviction that I must advance a Single-Issue Amendment in the hopes the LORD would grant a reprieve from His judgments and restore us to a God-fearing people once again.

What I did not foresee was the ignorance of many Educators and State Legislators I met, who had a poor regard for America's history, Constitution and the Article V process.

Article V of the United States Constitution

> "The Congress, whenever two-thirds of both Houses shall deem it necessary, shall propose Amendments to this Constitution, or, on the Application of the Legislatures of two-thirds of the several States, shall call a Convention for proposing Amendments, which, in either Case, shall be valid to all Intents and Purposes, as Part of this Constitution, when ratified by the Legislatures of three-fourths of the several States, or by Conventions in three-fourths thereof, as the one or the other Mode of Ratification may be proposed by the Congress; Provided that no Amendment which may be made prior to the Year One thousand eight hundred and eight shall in any Manner affect the first and fourth Clauses in the Ninth

Section of the first Article; and that no State, without its Consent, shall be deprived of its equal Suffrage in the Senate."

Two Methods of Ratification

Article V allows for two methods of proposing amendments:

a. Congress can propose amendments by a two-thirds majority vote in both the House of Representatives and the Senate.
b. State legislatures can direct Congress to convene an Amendment convention to propose amendments if two-thirds of them agree.

Ratification of an Amendment

To become part of the United States Constitution, it must be ratified by three-fourths of the State Legislatures or by conventions in three-fourths of the states.

Text of proposed
COUNTERMAND AMENDMENT
ARTICLE 28
(or alternate number to be assigned by Congress)

Section 1. The Article restores State sovereignty in our Constitutional Republic by providing State Legislatures Countermand authority.

Section 2. State Legislatures in the several States shall have the authority to Countermand and rescind any Congressional Statute, Judicial decision, Executive Order, Treaty, government agency's regulatory ruling, or any other government or non-government mandate (including excessive spending and credit) imposed on them when in the opinion of 60 percent of State Legislatures, the law or ruling adversely affects their States' interest. When the Countermand threshold has been reached, the law or ruling shall be immediately and automatically nullified and repealed. This Countermand authority shall also apply to existing laws and rulings.

Section 3. From the time the initial Countermand is issued by a State Legislature, the other Legislatures shall have eighteen months to complete the Countermand process. If the Countermand process is not completed in eighteen months, then the law or ruling that is being challenged shall remain enforceable.

Section 4. Each State Legislature must complete their Countermand affidavit and deliver a certified copy to the Chief Justice of the United States Supreme Court, the Leader of the United States Senate, the Speaker of the House of Representatives, the President of the United States, and when applicable the Government Agency or Body that is being challenged.

Section 5. Any elected or non-elected government official, or any non-government individual or organization, who intentionally obstructs or prevents the implementation of any provision in this Article shall have committed a criminal offense and shall be subject to impeachment (when applicable) and criminal prosecution and upon conviction serve up to five years in prison.

Section 6. Individual States shall have authority to prosecute violators of this Article under State laws in the absence of Federal prosecution after ninety days from the date of the alleged violation. Multiple prosecutions, by multiple States, for the same alleged crime are prohibited.

Section 7. The Article shall be immediately part of the United States Constitution upon ratification by three quarters of the State Legislatures in the several States.

Section 8. The provisions of this Article are enforceable within the United States which shall include the Several States, the District of Columbia, the Commonwealth of Puerto Rico, the Commonwealth of the Northern Mariana Islands and the territories and possessions of the United States.

I knew that the Countermand Amendment would not outlaw Roe V. Wade in the fifty States and Territories, but my reasoning was it may slow down the rate of abortions. At this point, I was worn out, and willing to spend what years I may have left to try and save some babies.

Joyce and I agreed to do our best to advance the Countermand Amendment in State Legislatures.

Countermand Amendment Exploratory Committee

We formed the 'Countermand Amendment Exploratory Committee'. I have been privileged to work with some of the greatest patriots America has produced. We labored for months to write the Countermand Amendment. I traveled to thirty-eight State Legislatures, sleeping in my car and in a travel home. Not one of our Directors received a penny for their patriotic labors.

My travels, over several years, allowed me to meet and befriend many State Legislators who are outstanding patriots.

Alaska, the First State to Make the Call on Congress

Alaska was the first State to approve the Article 5 Countermand Amendment. Our Alaska Director is a fellow veteran who worked tirelessly to secure approval from his State Legislature. He succeeded, and Alaska made the first Call on Congress to Call for the Article 5 Countermand Amendment Convention.

As many as fifteen other States were processing our Countermand Amendment proposal before my time, traveling to State Legislatures, ran out. My health was failing.

Meeting With State Legislators

My wife and State Directors would arrange my appointments with State legislators, Caucuses, Committees, and one on one legislator meetings. Over several years, I traveled to some State Legislatures multiple times.

I visited the North Dakota Legislature three times. Always in January—temperatures would drop to twenty degrees below zero. My State Director in South Dakota provided me with a travel home. Unfortunately, the heater did not work—it was extremely cold sleeping at night. I became ill and had to return to North Carolina after my third visit.

The North Dakota Senate scheduled a special Committee meeting for me to answer their questions. One Senator asked me, 'Would the population in California (forty million) give them greater voting power in the Amendment process.' North Dakota has a population of one million. I told him and the Committee, 'No, Article V gives each State in our Republic an equal vote regardless of populations. The Countermand Amendment also gives each State only one vote when countermanding a Federal law, statute or Court decision.' The Senate approved our Call on Congress, with, I believe, 98% of the Senators voting, Yay!

The North Dakota House approved the Countermand Amendment earlier, but decided they needed to reconcile the differences between its version and the Senate's. The House approved the 'Convention of States' Article 5 Convention Call which called for a Convention without State Legislature controls. I was contacted by their Executive Director and asked if I would join their Committee.

I asked him two questions:

- a. Would the State Legislatures be able to write the Amendment before the Convention; and
- b. Would they be able to control the deliberations at the Convention with a 'Delegate Resolution.'

Both of these were already written and approved by Alaska.

The Executive Director said, 'No, to both questions.'

My answer was, 'No, I cannot join your Committee. Sovereignty of State Legislatures was paramount in our initiative. Article 5 is not for convening a Constitutional Convention that Convention of States was originally calling for. It later modified their language to make it appear that the delegates would have a modicum of accountability to their State Legislatures.

Article 5 is for Calling on Congress to convene a Single-Issue Amendment Convention, thus preserving our original Constitutional documents and Republic. Delegates sent to Single-Issue Amendment Conventions are Ambassadors of their State Legislatures, not independent delegates who would be empowered to create a new Constitution.

Some 'So Called' Constitutional Scholars argued that an Article V Constitutional Convention Was Too Dangerous

This legal advice is based on an extremely flawed understanding of why our Founders gave us Article V in the first place.

When I was in law school, there was zero teaching on the Biblical principles our Founders used in writing the Declaration of Independence, Articles of Confederation, Constitution, and Bill of Rights. Virtually all the teaching in Law School was based on case law, statutory law, and regulatory rulings, written by men. Common Law, which carried a modicum of Biblical teaching was jettisoned. Students were given to understand that their only responsibility was to ignore Christian values and win their cases by twisting rules and decisions made by 'so called' legal experts. This secular approach, in defining America's laws, has degenerated even further to where today (fifty-five years later) it is nearly impossible to find Biblical values in any or our laws, or Constitution.

The Word of God tells us that the fear of the LORD is the beginning of wisdom, not the secular knowledge of men.

> *And you wonder why America has reached the bottom of the depravity barrel.*

The Article V Genius of our Founders

The Founders created, through much prayer, the *Article V Amendment Convention*, not a Constitutional Convention. They knew America needed only 'ONE' Constitutional Convention in 1776. They also knew that America would face egregious wrongs in the future that single issue amendments to the Constitution could remedy. Their genius is found in Article V. When used correctly, Congress and/or the State Legislatures could safely ratify a single-issue amendment that remedies any egregious wrong, without altering existing Rights and Privileges Americans have in the Constitution. One of our Leaders told me that if the State Legislatures adopted the Single-Issue Amendment process before 1860, we could have avoided the carnage in the Civil War (621,000 young men lost their lives in the Civil War that could have been avoided).

Again, I tell you that Article V does not authorize a 'Constitutional Convention'. It authorizes *Single-Issue Amendment Conventions* that are to be used in the same way our Bill of Rights was used when sending twelve Amendments to State Legislatures for ratification, after the Constitution was ratified by the States.

Go to: https: countermands.us for a complete discussion.

> *"It is impossible to rightly govern a nation without God and the Bible."*
>
> —George Washington

"... To the distinguished character of Patriot, it should be our highest glory to add the more distinguished character of Christian."

—George Washington

"... those general Principles of Christianity, are as eternal and immutable, as the Existence and Attributes of God; "

—John Adams

Chapter 16

Dietrich Bonhoeffer, Lutheran Pastor and Patriot

IT IS IMPORTANT FOR me to acknowledge that it was an Evangelical Lutheran Pastor (seventy-four years ago) who started me and my family on our Christian journey, Now, at the end of this book, acknowledging, Dietrich Bonhoeffer (one of the most faithful and heroic Christian men in the 20th Century) and another Evangelical Lutheran Pastor, was not planned.

Dietrich Bonhoeffer (4 February 1906—9 April 1945) was a German Lutheran pastor, theologian and anti-Nazi dissident who was a key founding member of the *Confessing Church*. His writings on Christianity's role in the secular world have become widely influential; his 1937 book *The Cost of Discipleship* is described as a modern classic. Apart from his theological writings, Bonhoeffer was known for his staunch resistance to the Nazi dictatorship, including vocal opposition to Adolf Hitler's euthanasia program and genocidal persecution of the Jews. He was arrested in April 1943 by the Gestapo and imprisoned at Tegel Prison for one and a half years. Later, he was transferred to Flossenbürg concentration camp.

Bonhoeffer was accused of being associated with the July 20 plot to assassinate Hitler and was tried along with other accused plotters, including former members of the Abwehr (the German Military Intelligence Office). He was hanged on 9 April 1945 during the collapse of the Nazi regime.

(Open source)

Confessing Church

The *Confessing Church* was a movement within German Protestantism during Nazi Germany. It emerged in opposition to government-sponsored efforts to unify all Protestant churches into a single pro-Nazi German Evangelical Church.

Background and Opposition

In the 1930's, Adolf Hitler attempted to manipulate the churches for Nazi propaganda and politics. The Confessing Church resisted this manipulation and sought to maintain its independence from state control. It rejected racial ideology as incompatible with Christianity.

Membership and Influence

The *Confessing Church* had around 3,000 pastors. It was the most significant institutional resistance to the Nazi dictatorship within Protestant churches. The movement emphasized faithfulness to biblical principles and opposed any compromise with Nazi ideology.

Barmen Declaration

In 1934, the *Confessing Church* issued the Barmen Declaration, which affirmed the primacy of Jesus Christ and rejected any allegiance to the Nazi regime.

The declaration emphasized that the church's loyalty was to God, not the state.

Persecution

Many pastors associated with the *Confessing Church* were arrested by Nazi authorities. Despite persecution, the movement continued to uphold its principles and resist Nazi influence.

The Confessing Church played a crucial role in maintaining Christian integrity during a dark period in German history. Its commitment to faithfulness and opposition to Nazi ideology remain significant examples of moral courage and resilience.

Germany's Constitutional Republic Lost

Dietrich Bonhoeffer was caught up in European chaos during the 30's and 40's. Germany had lost its Constitutional Republic and Hitler assumed dictatorial authority over all political and religious matters. Bonhoeffer, tried to organize opposition to Hitler and his regime.

Bonhoeffer, exercising his Christian faith, rejected Hitler's Nazi genocidal anti-Semitic propaganda.

Bonhoeffer and his handful of loyal Christian followers stood alone, and it cost them dearly.

> "Yea, and all that will live godly in Christ Jesus shall suffer persecution." (2 Timothy 3:12)

American Christians by Comparison

Germany never had the protections American Christians have had in our historical governing documents:

1. Mayflower Compact 1620
2. Articles of Confederation
3. Declaration of Independence
4. Constitution
5. Bill of Rights

Bonhoeffer stood with the LORD in opposition to unrighteousness. He took deliberate actions to confirm his convictions using faith, courage and Christian common sense. He opposed (with God's righteousness) the established government, in order to protect the LORD's Church and Jewish people from destruction at the hands of a Satanic Nazi regime.

I am persuaded that the LORD has been directing Christians in America to follow Dietrich Bonhoeffer's example and oppose all unrighteous laws and politics in America, while at the same time proclaiming the Gospel of Jesus Christ to the nations. Article 5 is the Constitutional authority given to Christians to protect the Unborn and our Christian heritage.

Chapter 17

My Wife's Final Days

Her children arise up, and call her blessed; her husband also, and he praiseth her. Many daughters have done virtuously, but thou excellest them all. Favour is deceitful, and beauty is vain: but a woman that feareth the LORD, she shall be praised. Give her of the fruit of her hands; and let her own works praise her in the gates." (Proverbs 31:27-31)

LOSING ONE'S WIFE TO cancer is a common suffering many husbands have experienced. In my experience, I have also lost a woman who loved the LORD dearly, her husband, children, grandchildren and many others.

Learning how to be a widower has proven to be a very difficult task.

A Dark Spot

I noticed a dark spot on Joyce's back, about the size of a quarter. I asked, 'Joyce, what is this dark spot?' She said, 'I don't know.' We agreed, it was time to seek the advice of a doctor.

After several preliminary doctor appointments, we were referred to an Oncologist.

The Oncologist began an examination and took tissue samples to confirm his suspicions that the black spot was cancer. The report from the tissue sample concluded that Joyce had an extremely aggressive strain of Melanoma Cancer. By this time, the small black spot grew to the size of a cantaloupe.

Weekly transfusions were ordered (to build up her immune system) in the hopes that the cancer's growth would slow down. They did not work.

Initially the Oncologist ordered twelve Xray treatments. They did not stop the growth of the cancer.

By this time, it was discovered she also had cancer on her breast. Surgery was scheduled for the cancer on her back. The preliminary report indicated that the cancer was removed, but there remained a possibility that it may have spread to other parts of the body.

A month later, the cancer on her back reappeared. This time it had grown to the size of a watermelon, covering the entire upper portion of her back.

Finally, Chemo treatments were ordered which did in fact destroy the cancer below her neck. Joyce had two PET Scans. They concluded that the cancer below her neck was gone.

Praising the LORD Together

Earlier, my wife said, Raymond, the LORD will heal me either down here or in heaven. My wife's faith and trust in the LORD was greater than mine.

Joyce was so excited believing the LORD healed her that she stood up at Church waving two PET Scan reports telling the whole Church what the LORD did for her. She mentioned just about everyone in the Church who ministered to her over the last year and a half, thanking them for their prayers, encouragement, and support. But she neglected to mention her husband. So, I stood up (having a little fun) and said, 'What about your husband?' The Pastor and congregation broke out in laughter.

Of course, I wasn't looking for recognition, but it seemed a perfect place to add some humor. Joyce immediately recognized my ministry to her and with gratitude I praised her. Again, the Church was laughing.

A few weeks went by, and Joyce began to get weaker. The cancer metastasized and traveled to her brain. The PET Scans did not scan her brain. Soon, I was no longer strong enough to carry her in and out of her wheelchair and from her bed to the bathroom.

We needed help and the LORD provided. In short stead, we had palliative and Hospice volunteers attending to her.

Less than two weeks later, Joyce's condition deteriorated badly. She was transferred to a long-term care facility. I stayed with her (day and night) trying to provide some comfort. I wept most of the time.

She had a Christian roommate, a 96-year-old lady who wanted to join the Bible studies Joyce and I were having. For a short while, the three of us had wonderful moments in prayer and readings in God's Word.

Her Body Was Shutting Down

The Doctor told us that her body was shutting down and there was nothing he could do to help her. He said they would try to keep her as comfortable as possible.

This was that time when I wept and wept and wept. Being married to the woman who knocked my socks off 60 years earlier and to see her now, after all we had been through, was more than I could bear.

She was moved into a private room for terminally ill patients. The extended care facility provided me with a recliner to sleep in her room at nights.

Throughout the night she would breathe heavily through her mouth. She was motionless.

She had already lost the use of her limbs, neck, and facial muscles. She was bald and unable to speak. I tried, in vain, to hold back tears as I watched her slowly die.

Trying to Cheer Her Up

Before she lost her ability to speak, I said to her, 'Joyce, I've been thinking about what it will be like when the two of us are in heaven. There's a possibility that the LORD is going to make you a General and me a Corporal. That doesn't sound much like heaven to me.' Joyce laughed, and we had a few precious moments realizing how much we meant to each other.

Changing Places With Her

Before she became terminal and while she was still able to hear and speak, I told her, 'Sweetheart, I would change places with you in a heartbeat, if I could.'

Are They Treating You Alright?

As I was caressing her arm, she was trying to say something, but I could not understand. I said, 'Joyce, let me get a pad and pen and maybe you will be able to write what you are trying to say.'

I put the pad under her right hand (there was still some movement in her fingers) and a pen between her fingers. She immediately began to scribble. Even though I tried to move the pad to help her write, everything she scribbled made no sense. I continued to look at the scribble on different parts of the paper, and then, all of a sudden, I saw what she was trying to say: 'Are you asking me if they are treating me alright?' She whispered, 'Yes'. I immediately told her, with tears, 'Yes, they are treating me well.'

Can you image being married to a woman who was hours away from death, and she is now concerned about how her husband is being treated by the medical facility she would soon die in. My wife was one of God's most graceful and beautiful Christian ladies in the Church. I thank the LORD frequently for God fearing, gracious, Christian ladies. They are God's greatest gift to Christian men.

Please, Relieve the Suffering

On April 25, 2023, I was pleading with the LORD to relieve my wife of her suffering. She was breathing hard and loud throughout the night. I can still picture her struggling to breathe and me not being able to help her.

At 4:25 A.M the room became silent. I looked over at Joyce and, in my mind's eye, saw an angel escorting her home. My wife, and fellow servant for the LORD, went home leaving behind a body that was lifeless. I found the head nurse and asked her to come to her room. The nurse pronounced her dead.

Remembering How I Pleaded With the LORD to Save My Wife 53 Years Earlier

In 1971, I pleaded with the LORD to give me a Christian wife. My prayer was:

> 'Lord, I don't care the cost—you can take my arm, even my life—but please, confirm to me Joyce's salvation.'

The LORD gave me the wife I prayed for without taking my arm or life. He gave the wife I needed to complete the work He appointed for me. Was she a perfect woman, no. Was I a perfect man, no. However, she was God's perfect woman for me. I wouldn't trade Joyce for a thousand others.

> "Oh LORD Jesus, you gave Joyce and me a journey filled with grief. Yes, there were moments of joy along the way that strengthened us and drew us closer to You. You answered our prayers for our children and grandchildren. You gave us ministries that led many to Jesus Christ. You gave us a love for your Unborn Children and our Christian heritage. And You also gave us the faith, resolve, burden for souls and your righteousness that carried us through 59 years. Bless you LORD for allowing Joyce and me to be a very small part of your redemptive plan throughout the ages. AMEN"

I Failed to Stop Abortion in America

After fifty-one years of labor, Joyce and I failed to stop abortion in America with the Article 5 Unborn Child Amendment.

We also failed to secure the required support from Congress and State Legislatures to ratify the Article 5 Countermand Amendment. Our Constitutional Republic and Christian heritage remain in jeopardy.

BUT...

Somehow, the LORD miraculously allowed Joyce and me to be His witnesses for Jesus Christ, to millions of people in seventy-four nations. The LORD greatly blessed us with a harvest of souls who will join us in heaven praising and worshiping Him forever.

> "And they that be wise shall shine as the brightness of the firmament; and they that turn many to righteousness as the stars for ever and ever." (Daniel 12:3)

Chapter 18

God's Favor Since My Wife's Death

It is now twelve months since my wife went home to be with our LORD. I miss her greatly. Remembering that the LORD gave me the desire of my heart by giving her to me and saving her, I remain greatly blessed.

Several close friends encouraged me to write this book. I was trying to put the idea out of my mind. I wasn't sure my memoirs would be of much interest to others. I also knew the effort it would take to complete the book.

Finally, I asked the LORD, 'Should I write a book of my memoirs and journey with Joyce?" It wasn't long before I concluded it was time to write this book.

Over the last six months, there have been many encouragements from strangers who after hearing my testimony, showed their favor by giving me hugs or paying for my meals.

Hug's After My Wife's Death

Here's a list of some of the Hugs I received (from mostly strangers) since Joyce died:

1. Often, I visit the Erwin Linear Trail in Tennessee. There is a paved path that separates a beautiful river on one side with ducks, geese, beavers, fish, etc. living freely in the wild; and on the other side, three beautiful lakes with more wild animals. One day, I was able to walk about 2/10th of a mile to a pedestrian bridge. There was a couple on the bridge in their late 30's. We greeted each other and a conversation started about my wife who died a few months earlier. I began to share my testimony of how I met my wife and what the LORD did, with the two of us, over our last 59 years together. About halfway through my testimony, I said, 'Maybe I'd better stop. I have taken too much of your time.' But the wife responded, no, no, I want to hear more. After sharing with her and her husband my story and especially how I asked the LORD for a thousand souls before I died, and instead He gave me 90,000, the wife looked at me and said, 'Before you go, can I give you a hug.'

    I said, 'Yes'. She walked over to me and gave me a bear hug. I thought to myself, how am I to understand this?

2. While at a restaurant, I shared my testimony, when a lady who was listening began to cry. No hugs though. WOW!

3. While having breakfast, the owner of a restaurant began to talk with me. She asked what I do. I began to tell her of my testimony and afterwards, she stood up and said, 'Can I give you a hug?' Now I am beginning to think the LORD has His hand in this.

4. One morning, while having breakfast, I looked across the room and saw eight ladies sitting at a table having a Bible Study. I said LORD, do you want me to go over there and tell

them the great blessing they are to me. One of the ladies had a little baby in her arms.

I introduced myself and said that they are gems among God's best. Their leader asked what I do which gave me an opportunity to once again share my testimony. Afterwards, she said, 'Is there something you would like us to pray for.' I said yes. Ministry Channels.

5. There were three people sitting at a table. As I walked behind them, I called out to the young woman who, after 15 years, remembered my handshake. One of the ladies at the table said, 'I would love to have dinner with you—if you are treating?'

   After a couple of friendly comments, they invited me to sit with them. They wanted to know what I did and that led to sharing my testimony. The three of them were professing Christians, but I don't think they were saved.

   After they politely listened to my wife's and my testimony, the 92 years of woman tried to get up to give me a hug. She was not able to stand, so she reached out her hand to shake mine and said, 'Keep being the man you are.' Our conversation, with the three of them, gave me a wonderful opportunity to clearly say how one comes to know Jesus Christ as their personal Savior.

6. While sharing my testimony with a woman who I knew from 20+ years earlier, she stood up and said, 'Ray, can I give you a hug.'

I think I may have missed one or two other encounters that belong in this list. What amazes me, just about all these encounters were with strangers.

I asked myself, what was the LORD trying to tell me? I enjoyed sharing my testimony of how I met Joyce and how the LORD blessed our lives over 59 years. But I never thought the LORD would send me such favor from strangers.

Meals Paid by Strangers After My Wife Died

Here's a list of some of the *'free meals'* I received (from mostly strangers) since Joyce died:

1. A man and his wife were sitting at an adjacent table to mine. We greeted each other and the husband asked what I do. I told Him I am an Evangelist and operate my own business.

   This broke the ice and they wanted to know more. When they heard that my wife recently passed away and the Christian testimony the LORD gave the two of us, they told the server that they will pay for my meal. I did not know this until I asked the server for my check. She said the couple I was sitting adjacent to paid my check.

2. One evening, I was sitting at a table next to a young teenager and her grandparents. We began a casual conversation that soon focused on their granddaughter. I felt the freedom to encourage their granddaughter in the LORD. Unbeknownst to me, another couple at another table, who I never talked with, paid for my meal.

3. I don't remember how this encounter started, but a man who was sitting with his own group, heard me talking with some friends at a separate table. He walked up to me and said, 'I want you to use this for your ministry.' It was $100.

4. Earlier in this book I told the story of a 20-year-old (with her husband) who shook my hand from left to right. This gave me a wonderful opportunity to engage them in the LORD, pray for them, and to encourage them to go on in ministry for Jesus.

   Afterwards, when I asked the server for my check, she said, 'The young couple paid for it.'

5. I was ordering my meal at a steak house, when a man came running over to tell the order taker that he wanted to pay for my meal. This man came out of the blue.

6. There have been other individuals who paid for my meals. I am overwhelmed by God's favor.

Realizing that all these events happened since my wife died, I am hesitant to conclude too much, other than the LORD has been trying to encourage me to write this book, and to continue to go on as a soul winning widower.

Chapter 19

Redeeming the Time

YEARS AGO, MY SON had this verse painted and framed as a mural. I have cherished it ever since. Often, I look on the wall where my wife hung it and prayerfully read it. The verse reminds me that we are acceptable for His service, no matter who we are, or how old we are.

Serving the LORD Until Our Last Breadth

> "O God, thou hast taught me from my youth: and hitherto have I declared thy wondrous works. Now also when I am old and grayheaded, O God, forsake me not; until I have shewed thy strength unto this generation, and thy power to everyone that is to come." (Psalm 71:7,18)

In Mark 9:44 our LORD tells us that there is a hell and that those who chose to go there suffer greatly:

Hell Is a Place of Torment

> "... it is better for thee to enter into life maimed, than having two hands to go into hell, into the fire that never shall be quenched: Where their worm dieth not, and the fire is not quenched." (Mark 9:44)

God Never Sends a Man to Hell

God never sends a man to hell. Each man has an equal opportunity to have his sins forgiven, but he first must recognize he is a sinner (separated from a holy God), and by himself he is helpless to remove his sin. Only the sacrificial blood of the Son of God can take away our sins. By faith alone, He gives men the pardon that is needed to enter heaven as a forgiven man.

> "For God so loved the world, that he gave his only begotten Son, that whosoever believeth in him should not perish, but have everlasting life. For God sent not his Son into the world to condemn the world; but that the world through him might be saved. He that believeth on him is not condemned: but <u>he that believeth not is condemned already</u>, because he hath not believed in the name of the only begotten Son of God. And this is the condemnation, that light is come into the world, and men loved darkness rather than light, because their deeds were evil. For every one that doeth evil hateth the light, neither cometh to the light, lest his deeds should be reproved. But he that doeth truth cometh to the light, that his deeds may be made manifest, that they are wrought in God." (John 3:16-21)

> "Wherefore seeing we also are compassed about with so great a cloud of witnesses, let us lay aside every weight, and the sin which doth so easily beset us, and let us run with patience the race that is set before us." (Hebrews 12:1)

> "And let us not be weary in well doing: for in due season we shall reap, if we faint not." (Galatians 6:9)

> "Holding forth the word of life; that I may rejoice in the day of Christ, that I have not run in vain, neither laboured in vain." (Philippians 2:16)

As I conclude the writing of this book, I leave the following with the reader:

If you want to be forgiven of your sins—with a humble and honest heart, offer the follow prayer to the LORD;

a. LORD Jesus, I have sinned against you.
b. I confess my sins and repent of them.
c. Please forgive me and make me a child of God.
d. Thank you, LORD, for forgiving me of my sins.
e. Seal me with your Holy Spirit and teach me to faithfully follow you.
f. AMEN

Congratulations, by reciting this prayer, you have been received into the Family of God. You are now a Born-Again Christian.

Ask the LORD to lead you to a Bible believing Church. Follow the LORD in Baptism. In Baptism you are declaring that you are not ashamed of the name Jesus Christ.

Start reading your Bible regularly. The LORD will reveal to you some very wonderful truths that will give you an understanding of the LORD's purposes for you and your future.

Keep in your mind that as a new creation in Jesus Christ, you have received special gifts and ministries that only you can use. Prayerfully, find a Church where your gifts would be a blessing to others.

If you are having trouble reciting the above prayer, offer the following to God with an honest heart:

I don't know who you are. Please help me in my unbelief.

The LORD will answer you directly.

About the Author

Charles Kacprowicz

Charles Kacprowicz is the Author of: Article V *'Unborn Child Amendment'*, *'Eleventh Nation—America Identified in Prophecy'*, *'Reclaiming America through Single Issue Federal Conventions'*, *'Countermand Amendment—the Missing Piece in the Article V Puzzle'*, and *'Defenders of the Unborn, Winners of Souls, Christian Patriots'*.

Charles is the Founder of: Citizen Initiatives, Ministry Channels Int'l, Internet Business Malls, Inc., and Markets Global USA, LLC.

He has also authored numerous white pages.

Restoring Our Constitutional Republic

He has been working for fifty-three years to restore our Constitutional Republic through Single Issue Article V Amendments that are to be initiated through Congress or State Legislatures. The Countermand Amendment has been his focus for many years. With it, Americans would be able to protect and restore our Constitutional Republic and Christian heritage by empowering State Legislatures to countermand and rescind laws and regulations that violate States Rights and/or our personal liberties, without altering our protections in the Constitution. The Countermand Amendment will allow State Legislatures to establish a Constitutionally correct balance of power between the Federal government and the States. The Federal government can rewrite a rescinded law or abandon it. If the government rewrites a law, it will have to do so in a way amenable to the States because it too can be countermanded.

Turning 90,000 people to Jesus Christ

Fifty-three years ago, Charles prayed asking the LORD not to allow him to see death until he leads at least 1,000 people to Jesus Christ. The LORD did not give Charles 1,000 souls, instead He gave him 90,000 souls in seventy-four nations—each one confirming that he/she said the sinners prayer to become a Christian.

> "O God, thou hast taught me from my youth: and hitherto have I declared thy wondrous works. Now also when I am old and gray headed, O God, forsake me not; until I have shewed thy strength unto this generation, and thy power to everyone that is to come." (Psalms 71:17,18)

> "And they that be wise shall shine as the brightness of the firmament; and they that turn many to righteousness as the stars for ever and ever." (Daniel 12:3)

Today Charles is working to send the Gospel Letter to upwards of a billion people in one hundred fifty-six nations representing upwards of 60% of the families in the world. The Gospel Letter tells the story of why the Son of God (Jesus Christ) came to earth and how men can be saved from their sin through childlike faith in Jesus Christ. Each Gospel Letter includes a digital study Bible in eighty languages, search tools, Hebrew and Greek texts, Strong's Concordance, commentaries, Lexicons, Topical Concordance, and a two-hour Jesus Film in 1,759 languages.

In the United States, new converts are to be forwarded to participating Evangelical Churches, to follow up and disciple. Charles' vision includes growing existing Churches and starting new ones in one hundred and fifty-six countries. The Gospel Letter reaches people in their workplace, at home, while traveling, and when relaxing. It reaches people on their wrist watches, cell phones, tabloids, and computers. It penetrates deep into every nation reaching people the Church cannot. Ministry Channels' cost for each new convert has been as little as thirty-five cents. The lowest cost per convert in any evangelical ministry.

Based on recent results, Ministry Channels International is able to forecast as many as 100,000 people becoming Christians every month through the Gospel Letter. The Church, in 2,000 years, has never had such an opportunity to reach the lost.

> "So shall My word be that goes forth from My mouth; It shall not return to Me void, But it shall accomplish what I please, And it shall prosper in the thing for which I sent it." (Isaiah 55:11)

Article V Unborn Child Amendment

Charles has been fighting for the Unborn Child's right to life since January 23, 1973. He is the Founder and National Director of Article V '*Unborn Child Amendment*. The Unborn Child is the father's heritage, America's heritage and God's heritage. The LORD is populating the earth and heaven with each new generation. When a child is aborted, future generations are never born, and God's heritage is lost forever.

> "Blessed is the nation whose God is the LORD, and the people whom He hath chosen for His own inheritance." (Psalm 33:12)

The 1st Paragraph of the United States Constitution reads as follows:

> "We the People of the United States, in Order to form a more perfect Union, establish Justice, ensure domestic Tranquility, provide for the common defense, promote the general Welfare, and secure the Blessings of Liberty to ourselves and *our Posterity*, do ordain and establish this Constitution for the United States of America."

The Unborn Child has always been identified as a person in our Constitution with the word 'Posterity'.

After hearing the news, on January 22, 1973, that the United States Supreme Court made elective abortions legal in its Roe vs. Wade decision, he addressed an outdoor audience at Akron, OH the following day. His message before the first elective abortion was performed:

> *"We must overturn Roe vs. Wade! . . . We must not give American woman the right to decide who lives and dies in America".*

Article V Single Issue Amendments

Charles personally met with hundreds of State legislators in thirty-eight States. He has spoken before many State Government Committees and Caucuses, appeared on radio and TV talk shows, has conducted prophecy seminars, been the guest speaker before two hundred audiences, and lobbied Congress on behalf of the *Unborn Child Amendment* and Late Term Abortion Bill twice vetoed by President Clinton. He has received support from United States Senators, State Legislators, Church leaders, and Pro-Life Groups. He also founded and hosted the radio talk show *State Legislators Round Table*.

Sixty-Five Years of Service and Ministry

Charles has served in the Church as Preacher, Evangelist, Elder, Deacon, Teacher, Jail Ministry Chaplain, Youth Director, and is a member of Bethel Missionary Baptist Church. He has been recognized by Entrepreneur Magazine for founding one of America's top five hundred entrepreneurial companies, has been licensed by the National Association of Security Dealers (NASD), and has been awarded the coveted "Authority Author" by Ezine Directories. He presently owns and operates Markets Global USA, LLC, a company that focuses on 'Market Niche Penetration Strategies'. He founded and operated Internet Business Malls, Inc. with 50 employees, operating in fifty States. The company's mission was to create an online presence, exclusively for businesses, through interactive capabilities that defined Industries and subsets by eight digit SIC Codes.

Charles was born in 1941, was married to his late wife, Joyce Roschy Casper, for fifty-eight years, has two sons and nine grandchildren. He's a graduate of California State University, with 4½ years of post- graduate work at Loyola Law School and Moody Bible Extension Studies. He is a service-connected disabled veteran and served honorably in the U.S. Navy from 1958 to 1964 (includes two years in Naval Reserves.)

Ministry Channels International
Reaching the Unreached
P.O. Box 523
Spruce Pine, NC 28777

ABOUT THE AUTHOR

(828) 385 2438
https://ministrychannels.org
info@ministrychannels.org
https://ministrychannels.org/gospel-letter/

www.ingramcontent.com/pod-product-compliance
Lightning Source LLC
Chambersburg PA
CBHW071211160426
43196CB00011B/2257